Easy Spanish Phrase Book

Alex Torres

MONKEY
PUBLISHING

OUR HAND-PICKED
BOOK SELECTION FOR YOU.

LEARN
SOMETHING NEW
EVERYDAY.

ISBN: 9798524299130

Table of Contents

Introduction

Whether you're visiting another country for business or leisure, it's very useful to know the basics of the language. Learning a few phrases can make a holiday more enjoyable, make a great impression with the locals, or even get you out of a tricky situation. Simply being able to order your favorite drink in a bar, or ask directions to the train station, can make all the difference to your trip.

This phrasebook is packed full of useful, commonly used phrases, divided into handy sections for different circumstances. You'll have phrases at your fingertips whenever you need them. From booking a hotel room or hiring a car to phrases you can use to strike up a conversation or find help in an emergency. This one book is all you need.

While the Spanish alphabet looks very similar to English, there are several differences when it comes to pronunciation. So to make this easier for you, we've provided you with an additional phonetic version of each phrase, just say what you see, adding emphasis where the text is underlined. Please note that when a word contains just one syllable, the entire word should be emphasised, however we have not underlined all these words for clarity of reading the text. We've used a phonetics system that is aimed at English speakers as opposed to official phonetic translations that can be difficult to understand.

But if you'd like to learn more, to ensure your Spanish pronunciation is spot on, read on…

A Guide to Spanish Pronunciation

As with English, the Spanish language has five vowels, A, E, I, O, and U. Each vowel has a distinct sound. It is always pronounced the same way, and it's worth remembering, if you want to perfect your accent, that vowels in Spanish have a set length, and are usually shorter than their English counterparts. Also, if there is an accent on any vowel, this vowel should be emphasised in your pronunciation.

Let's take a closer look at vowels

A - The vowel A is pronounced 'ah', like the a in 'father'.
E – E is pronounced as 'eh', like the e in 'bed'.
I – The letter I is pronounced as 'ee' as in 'see'.
O – O is simply pronounced as 'oh', just like 'know', so now you know how to pronounce O.
U – U is pronounced as a short 'uu'. Like the u in 'put'.

Tackling the consonants

Many consonants in Spanish are pronounced very similarly to how they are pronounced in English, but there are several exceptions. It's worth learning the more common ones to really help you get your phrases across clearly. Here are some of the consonant sounds that are rather different to how you might expect…

H – The letter H is nearly always silent. There is no sound for the letter H in Spanish, so you would never have a word such as 'hat', it would be pronounced as 'at'. However, some words from other languages have been brought into common use and for these, the letter H is pronounced like the Spanish letter J.

J – On the other hand, the letter J is pronounced like the letter H in English. So if English followed the same rules, the name Jack would be pronounced as Hack.

G – The pronunciation of the letter G is dependant on the letter that follows it. If G is before either E or I then it is pronounced like the letter H. When followed by any other letter, then you simply pronounce it as you would the G in 'garden'.

Some more subtle differences...

B – The letter B is pronounced the same as in English, but it is always said softly, resulting in a sound similar to the letter V.

R – R is also pronounced very softly, sometimes almost sounding like a letter D.

D – The letter D should be pronounced with your tongue further forward in your mouth than you would usually have it to pronounce the letter D. The resulting sound is something close to a 'th' sound.

Q – Q is always pronounced like the letter K in English.

Z – The letter Z is pronounced like the letter S in English. ie. the word 'zoo' would sound like 'soo'.

There are also some consonants that are not present in the English alphabet...

LL – This letter is often pronounced like the letter Y, as in 'yoga', however in some countries, such as Argentina, Uruguay and parts of Chile, it is pronounced as 'sh'.

Ñ – Similar to N, but with more of a 'nyer' sound, Ñ is pronounced like the letters NY in the word 'canyon'.

RR – RR only occurs in the middle of a sentence and is simply pronounced like the letter R in 'red'.

Questions

Just like in English, questions in Spanish may be answered with a Yes or No. You'll realise when this is the case when the speaker raises the pitch of their voice at the end of the question.

¿Hablas español?		Do you speak Spanish?
Sí	*See*	Yes
No	*Noh*	No

Here are the words that form questions that require an answer beyond Yes or No. By learning them, you'll be able to find your way around in Spanish speaking countries.

Who?	¿Quién?	*Kee-ehn*
What?	¿Qué?	*Keh*
When?	¿Cuándo?	*Kwahn-doh*
Where?	¿Dónde?	*Dohn-deh*
Why?	¿Por qué?	*Pohr keh*
How?	¿Cómo?	*Cohm-mo*

Common Questions

Who are you?
> ¿Quién eres?
>> *¿Kee-ehn eh-rehs?*

What is your name?
> ¿Cuál es tu nombre?
>> *¿Kwahl ehs too nohm-breh?*

Whose is [it]?
> ¿De quién es [eso]?
>> *¿Deh kee-ehn ehs [eh-soh]?*

What is it?
> ¿Qué es eso?
>> *¿Keh ehs eh-soh?*

What are you doing now?
> ¿Qué haces ahora?
>> *¿Keh ah-sehs ah-oh-rah?*

When are you coming?
> ¿Cuándo vienes?
>> *¿Kwahn-doh vee-eh-nehs?*

When is your birthday?
> ¿Cuándo es tu cumpleaños?
>> *¿Kwahn-doh ehs too coom-pleh-ah-nyos?*

Where do you live?
> ¿Dónde vives?
>> *¿Dohn-deh vee-vehs?*

Where do you go?
> ¿A dónde vas?
>> *¿Ah dohn-deh vahs?*

Where are you from?
> ¿De dónde eres?
>> *¿Deh dohn-deh eh-rehs?*

Where do you work?
> ¿Dónde trabajas?
>> *¿Dohn-deh trah-bah-hahs?*

Why did you come here?

¿Por qué viniste aquí?

¿Pohr keh vee-nees-teh ah-kee?

How are you doing?

¿Cómo estás?

¿Coh-moh ehs-tahs?

How did you get here?

¿Cómo llegaste hasta aquí?

¿Coh-moh yeh-gahs-tah ahs-tah ah-kee?

How many hours until your next flight?

¿Cuántas horas faltan para el próximo vuelo?

¿Kwahn-tahs oh-rahs fahl-than pah-rah ehl prohx-see-moh bweh-loh?

How much is a bottle of water?

¿Cuánto sale una botella de agua?

¿Kwahn-toh sah-leh oo-nah boh-teh-yah deh ah-wa?

Can I ask you a question?

¿Puedo hacerte una pregunta?

¿Pwe-doh ah-sehr-teh oo-nah pre-goon-tah?

Days of the Week

Monday	Lunes	*Loo-nehs*
Tuesday	Martes	*Mahr-tehs*
Wednesday	Miércoles	*Mee-ehr-coh-lehs*
Thursday	Jueves	*Hoo-eh-vehs*
Friday	Viernes	*Vee-ehr-nehs*
Saturday	Sábado	*Sah-bah-doh*
Sunday	Domingo	*Doh-meen-goh*

Months

January	Enero	*Eh-neh-roh*
February	Febrero	*Feh-breh-roh*
March	Marzo	*Mahr-soh*
April	Abril	*Ah-breel*
May	Mayo	*Mah-yoh*
June	Junio	*Hoo-nyo*
July	Julio	*Hoo-lee-oh*
August	Agosto	*Ah-gohs-toh*
September	Septiembre	*Sehp-tee-ehm-breh*
October	Octubre	*Ohs-too-breh*
November	Noviembre	*Noh-vee-ehm-breh*
December	Diciembre	*Dee-see-ehm-breh*

Numbers

Cardinal Numbers

0	Cero	*Seh-roh*
1	Uno	*Oo-no*
2	Dos	*Dohs*
3	Tres	*Trehs*
4	Cuatro	*Kwah-troh*
5	Cinco	*Seen-coh*
6	Seis	*Seh-ees*
7	Siete	*See-eh-teh*
8	Ocho	*Oh-cho*
9	Nueve	*Noo-eh-veh*
10	Diez	*Dee-ehs*
11	Once	*Ohn-seh*
12	Doce	*Doh-seh*
13	Trece	*Treh-seh*
14	Catorce	*Cah-tohr-seh*
15	Quince	*Keen-seh*
16	Dieciséis	*Dee-eh-see-seh-ess*
17	Diecisiete	*Dee-eh-see-see-eh-teh*
18	Dieciocho	*Dee-eh-see-oh-choh*
19	Diecinueve	*Dee-eh-see-noo-eh-veh*
20	Veinte	*Veh-een-teh*
21	Veintiuno	*Veh-een-tee-oo-noh*
22	Veintidos	*Veh-een-tee-dohs*
23	Veintitres	*Veh-een-tee-oo-trehs*
30	Treinta	*Treh-een-tah*
40	Cuarenta	*Kwah-rehn-tah*

50	Cincuenta	*Seen-kwehn-tah*
60	Sesenta	*Seh-sehn-tah*
70	Setenta	*Seh-tehn-tah*
80	Ochenta	*Oh-chen-tah*
90	Noventa	*Noh-vehn-tah*
100	Cien	*See-ehn*
200	Doscientos	*Dohs-see-ehn-tohs*
1000	Mil	*Meal*

Ordinal Numbers

First	Primero	*Pree-meh-roh*
Second	Segundo	*Seh-goon-doh*
Third	Tercero	*Tehr-seh-roh*
Fourth	Cuarto	*Kwahr-toh*
Fifth	Quinto	*Keen-toh*
Sixth	Sexto	*Sex-toh*
Seventh	Séptimo	*Sehp-tee-moh*
Eighth	Octavo	*Ohc-tah-voh*
Ninth	Noveno	*Noh-veh-noh*
Tenth	Décimo	*Deh-see-moh*

Telling the Time

What time is it?
¿Qué hora es?
¿Keh oh-rah ehs?

Can you tell me what time it is?
¿Puedes decirme la hora?
¿Pwe-dehs deh-seer-meh lah oh-rah?

It's 4 pm.
Son las 4 de la tarde.
Sohn lahs kwah-troh deh lah tahr-deh.

O' clock.
… en punto
… ehn poon-toh

Half past…
… y media/y treinta
… ee meh-dee-ah/ ee treh-een-tah

Quarter past…
… y cuarto
… e kwahr-toh

A quarter to…
… menos cuarto
… meh-nos kwahr-toh

Midnight
Medianoche
Meh-dee-ah-noh-cheh

Morning
Mañana
Mah-nya-nah

Noon
Mediodía
Meh-dee-oh-dee-ah

Afternoon
Tarde
Tahr-deh

Evening

Noche

Noh-cheh

At what time do you have class?

¿A qué hora tienes clase?

¿A keh oh-rah tee-ehn-ehs clah-seh?

My classes start at 7:00 in the morning.

Mis clases empiezan a las 7:00 de la mañana.

Mees clah-sehs ehm-pee-eh-sahn ah lahs see-eh-teh deh lah mah-nya-nah

Could we have lunch at 2:30 in the afternoon?

¿Podríamos almorzar a las dos y media de la tarde?

¿Poh-dree-ah-mohs ahl-mohr-sahr ah lahs dohs ee meh-dee-a deh lah tahr-deh?

I go to sleep around 11:00 at night.

Yo me duermo alrededor de las 11:00 de la noche.

Yoh meh doo-ehr-moh ahl-reh-deh-dohr deh lahs ohn-seh deh lah noh-cheh

Her appointment is at noon.

Su cita es al mediodía.

Soo see-tah ehs al meh-dee-oh-dee-ah

We'll go hiking tomorrow.

Mañana iremos de excursión.

Mah-nya-nah ee-reh-mohs deh ehx-coor-see-ohn

I couldn't sleep last night.

No pude dormir anoche.

Noh poo-deh dohr-meer ah-noh-cheh

Popular Colors

Green	Verde	*Vehr-deh*
Yellow	Amarillo	*Ah-mah-ree-yoh*
Blue	Azul	*Ah-sool*
White	Blanco	*Blahn-coh*
Light blue	Celeste	*Seh-lehs-teh*
Gold	Dorado	*Doh-rah-doh*
Gray	Gris	*Grees*
Brown	Marrón	*Mah-rohn*
Orange	Naranja	*Nah-rahn-hah*
Black	Negro	*Neh-groh*
Red	Rojo	*Roh-hoh*
Pink	Rosa	*Roh-sah*
Purple	Púrpura	*Poor-poo-rah*

What color is the car?
    ¿De qué color es el coche?
        ¿Deh keh coh-lohr ehs ehl coh-che?

The car is gray.
    El coche es gris.
        Ehl coh-che ehs grees

What is your favorite color?
    ¿Cuál es tu color favorito?
        ¿Kwahl ehs tu coh-lohr fah-voh-ree-toh?

My favorite color is red.
    Mi color favorito es el rojo.
        Mi coh-lohr fah-voh-ree-toh ehs ehl roh-hoh

What color is her hair?
    ¿De qué color es su pelo?
        ¿Deh keh coh-lohr ehs soo peh-loh?

Her hair is black.

Su pelo es negro.

Soo peh-loh ehs neh-groh

Do you like the green or the yellow shirt?

¿Te gusta la camisa verde o la amarilla?

¿Teh goos-tah lah cah-mee-sah vehr-deh oh lah a-mah-ree-yah?

I like the green one.

Me gusta la verde.

Me goos-tah lah vehr-deh

This is a red pen.

Es un bolígrafo rojo.

Ehs oon boh-lee-grah-foh roh-hoh

Greetings

Hello.
Hola.
Oh-lah

How are you?
¿Qué tal?
¿Keh tahl?

What's up?
¿Qué pasa?
¿Keh pah-sah?

How're you doing?
¿Cómo te va?
¿Coh-moh teh vah?

How is your day?
¿Qué tal tu día?
¿Keh tahl too dee-ah?

How is everything?
¿Cómo va todo?
¿Coh-moh vah toh-doh?

How is life?
¿Cómo va tu vida?
¿Coh-moh vah too vee-dah?

I'm great.
Estoy estupendo.
Ehs-toy ehs-too-pehn-doh

I'm very well.
Estoy muy bien.
Ehs-toy mooy bee-ehn

I'm okay.
Estoy bien.
Ehs-toy bee-ehn

I'm unwell.
Estoy mal.
Ehs-toy mahl

I feel terrible.

Estoy fatal.

Ehs-toy fah-tahl

I'm tired.

Estoy cansado.

Ehs-toy cahn-sah-doh

I'm exhausted.

Estoy exhausto.

Ehs-toy ex-sah-oos-toh

I'm sick.

Estoy enfermo.

Ehs-toy ehn-fehr-moh

And you?

¿Y tú?

¿Ee too?

Goodbye.

Adiós.

Ah-dee-ohs

See you tomorrow.

Nos vemos mañana.

Nohs veh-mohs mah-nya-nah

See you later.

Hasta luego.

Ahs-tah loo-eh-goh

See you soon, friend.

Hasta pronto, amigo.

Ahs-tah prohn-toh, ah-mee-goh

I have to go.

Tengo que irme.

Tehn-go keh eer-meh

I need to get going.

Necesito irme.

Neh-ceh-see-toh eer-meh

It's time for me to go!

¡Es hora de que me vaya!

Ehs <u>oh</u>-rah deh keh meh <u>vah</u>-ya

Speak soon.
Hablamos pronto.
Ah-<u>blah</u>-mohs <u>prohn</u>-toh

See you later!
¡Nos vemos!
¡Nohs <u>veh</u>-mohs!

It was so nice to meet you!
¡Me encantó conocerte!
Meh ehn-cahn-<u>toh</u> coh-noh-<u>sehr</u>-teh

I hope to see you soon.
Espero verte pronto.
Ehs-<u>peh</u>-roh <u>ver</u>-teh <u>prohn</u>-toh

May I introduce you to my friend?
¿Puedo presentarte a mi amigo?
¿<u>Pwe</u>-doh preh-sehn-<u>tahr</u>-teh ah mee ah-<u>mee</u>-goh?

Emotions

I'm happy.	Estoy contento/a.	*Ehs-toy cohn-tehn-toh/ah*
I'm sad.	Estoy triste.	*Ehs-toy trees-teh*
I'm scared.	Tengo miedo.	*Tehn-goh mee-eh-doh*
I'm excited.	Estoy emocionado/a.	*Ehs-toy eh-moh-see-oh-nah-doh/ah*
I'm bored.	Estoy aburrido/a.	*Ehs-toy a-boo-ree-doh/ah*
I'm angry.	Estoy enojado/a.	*Ehs-toy eh-noh-hah-doh/ah*
I love it.	Me encanta.	*Meh ehn-cahn-tah*
I like it.	Me gusta.	*Meh goos-tah.*
I don't like it.	No me gusta.	*Noh meh goos-tah*
I hate it.	Lo detesto.	*Loh deh-tehs-toh*
Cool!	¡Genial!	*¡Heh-nee-ahl!*
I don't care.	Me da igual.	*Meh da ee-goo-ahl*
As you wish.	Como quieras.	*Coh-moh kee-eh-rahs*
It bothers me.	Me molesta.	*Meh moh-lehs-tah*
I'm nervous.	Estoy nervioso/a.	*Ehs-toy nehr-vee-oh-soh/ah*
I'm sleepy.	Tengo sueño.	*Tehn-goh soo-eh-nyo*
I'm embarrassed.	Estoy avergonzado/a.	*Ehs-toy ah-ver-gohn-sah-doh/dah*
I'm calm.	Estoy tranquilo/a.	*Ehs-toy trahn-kee-loh/ah*
I'm jealous.	Estoy celoso/a.	*Ehs-toy ceh-loh-soh/ah*
I'm worried.	Estoy preocupado/a.	*Ehs-toy preh-oh-coo-pah-doh/ah*
I'm	Estoy agobiado/a.	*Ehs-toy ah-goh-bee-*

overwhelmed.		*ah-doh/ah*
I'm uncomfortable.	Estoy incómodo/a.	*Ehs-toy een-coh-moh-doh/ah*
I'm depressed.	Estoy deprimido/a.	*Ehs-toy deh-pree-mee-doh/ah*
I'm busy.	Estoy ocupado/a.	*Ehs-toy oh-coo-pah-doh/ah*
I'm shy.	Soy tímido/a.	*Soy tee-mee-doh/ah*
I'm sensitive.	Soy sensible.	*Soy sehn-see-bleh*

Common Sayings

Well dressed for a special occasion
De punta en blanco
Deh poon-tah ehn blahn-coh

To be right, to be assertive
Dar en el blanco
Dahr ehn ehl blahn-coh

To be or see everything with excessive optimism
Ver todo color de rosa
Ver toh-doh coh-lohr deh roh-sah

To look for the perfect man
Buscar el príncipe azul
Boos-cahr el preen-see-peh ah-sool

To belong to a royal or very rich family
Tener sangre azul
Teh-nehr sahn-greh ah-sool

To find the perfect or ideal partner
Encontrar tu media naranja
Ehn-cohn-trahr too meh-dee-ah nah-rahn-hah

To feel very embarrassed about something
Ponerse rojo como un tomate
Poh-nehr-seh roh-hoh coh-moh oon toh-mah-teh

There is no comparison
No hay color
No I coh-lohr

To have bad luck
Tener la negra
Teh-nehr la neh-grah

To have excellent vision
Tener vista de lince
Teh-nehr bees-tah deh leen-seh

To have a bad memory
Tener memoria de pez
Teh-nehr meh-moh-ree-ah deh pez

To be good for nothing
Ser la oveja negra
Sehr la oh-beh-hah neh-grah

To be a coward
Ser un gallina
Sehr oon gah-yee-nah

To trick someone, to rip someone off
Dar gato por liebre
Dahr gah-toh pohr lee-eh-breh

To be crazy
Estar como una cabra
Ehs-tahr coh-moh oo-nah cah-brah

A treacherous person, a person who cheats or mocks another one
Ser una rata
Sehr oo-nah rah-tah

To be a very lucky person
Tener más vidas que un gato
Teh-nehr mahs vee-dahs keh oon gah-toh

To be cunning and sharp in practical matters
Ser más astuto que un zorro
Sehr mahs ahs-too-toh keh oon soh-roh

To be a piece of cake
Ser pan comido
Sehr pan coh-mee-doh

To be eye candy
Ser un bombón
Sehr oon bohm-bohn

To be from another era
Ser del año de la pera
Sehr dehl a-nyo deh lah peh-rah

To turn the tables
Dar la vuelta a la tortilla
Dahr lah bwehl-tah a la torh-tee-yah

Do not care, couldn't care less

25

No importar un pepino/rábano
Noh eem-pohr-<u>tahr</u> oon peh-<u>pee</u>-noh/<u>rah</u>-bah-noh

To be a blockhead
Ser un melón
Sehr oon meh-<u>lohn</u>

To be the goose that lays the golden eggs
Ser la gallina de los huevos de oro
Sehr la gah-<u>yee</u>-nah deh lohs <u>oo-eh</u>-vohs deh <u>oh</u>-roh

To be here, there and everywhere
Estar hasta en la sopa
Ehs-<u>tahr</u> <u>ahs</u>-tah ehn lah <u>soh</u>-pah

To eat (one's) lunch
Comer la papa
Coh-<u>mehr</u> lah <u>pah</u>-pah

To put your foot in it
Meter la pata
Meh-<u>tehr</u> lah <u>pah</u>-tah

Without rhyme or reason
No tener pies ni cabeza
No teh-<u>nehr</u> pee-ehs nee cah-<u>beh</u>-sah

Without sleeping a wink
No pegar un ojo
Noh peh-<u>gahr</u> oon ojo

To walk on eggshells
Andar con pies de plomo
An-<u>dahr</u> cohn pee-ehs deh <u>ploh</u>-moh

To be in trouble, or up to one's neck
Con la soga al cuello
Cohn lah <u>soh</u>-gah ahl <u>kweh</u>-yoh

To cost a fortune, to cost an arm and a leg
Costar un ojo de la cara
Cohs-<u>tahr</u> oon <u>o</u>-hoh deh lah <u>cah</u>-rah

To not mince your words
Sin pelos en la lengua
Seen <u>peh</u>-lohs ehn lah <u>lehn</u>-wa

To be sick to death, to be fed up
Estar hasta las narices
Ehs-tahr ahs-tah lahs nah-ree-sehs

To be spot on
Dar en el clavo
Dahr ehn ehl clah-voh

To rest on your laurels
Dormirse en los laureles
Dohr-meer-seh ehn lohs lah-oo-reh-lehs

Between a rock and a hard place
Entre la espada y la pared
Ehn-treh lah ehs-pah-dah ee lah pah-rehd

To hit two birds with one stone
Matar dos pájaros de un tiro
Mah-tahr dohs pah-jah-rohs deh oon tee-roh

To be hard-pressed
A duras penas
Ah doo-rahs peh-nahs

To fly off the handle
Perder los estribos
Peh-dehr lohs ehs-tree-bohs

An act of good faith
De buena fe
Deh boo-eh-nah feh

To be nuts, or have a screw loose
Faltarle un tornillo
Fahl-tahr-leh oon tohr-nee-yoh

To cross the line
Pasarse de la raya
Pah-sahr-seh deh lah rah-yah

To get away with
Salirse con la suya
Sah-leer-seh cohn lah soo-yah

Getting to Know Someone

My name is...
Me llamo...
Meh yah-moh...

What's your name?
¿Cómo te llamas?
¿Coh-moh teh yah-mahs?

Nice to meet you.
Mucho gusto.
Moo-choh goos-toh

A pleasure.
Un placer.
Oon plah-sehr

Likewise.
Igualmente.
Ee-gooahl-mehn-teh

Where are you from?
¿De dónde eres?
¿De dohn-deh eh-rehs?

I'm from...
Soy de...
Soy deh...

How old are you?
¿Cuántos años tienes?
¿Kwahn-tohs a-nyos tee-eh-nehs?

I'm ... years old.
Tengo ... años.
Tehn-goh ... a-nyos.

I am American / an Englishman / an Englishwoman.
Soy estadounidense / inglés(a).
Soy ehs-tah-doh-oo-nee-dehn-seh/een-glehs(a)

What do you do (for work)?
¿A qué te dedicas?
¿A keh teh deh-dee-cahs?

28

I'm a teacher / student / doctor.
>Soy profesor(a) / estudiante / doctor(a).
>>*Soy proh-feh-<u>sohr(a)</u>/ehs-too-<u>dee-ahn</u>-teh/doh-<u>tohr(ah)</u>*

What do you like to do in your free time?
>¿Qué te gusta hacer en tu tiempo libre?
>>*¿Keh teh <u>goos</u>-tah ah-<u>sehr</u> ehn too <u>tee-ehm</u>-poh <u>lee</u>-breh?*

I like to watch movies / to read / to dance.
>Me gusta ver películas / leer / bailar.
>>*Meh <u>goos</u>-tah vehr peh-<u>lee</u>-coo-lahs / lehr / bah-ee-<u>lahr</u>*

What's your favorite movie / book / band?
>¿Cuál es tu película favorita / libro favorito / banda favorita?
>>*¿Kwahl ehs too peh-<u>lee</u>-coo-lah fah-voh-<u>ree</u>-tah / <u>lee</u>-broh fah-voh-<u>ree</u>-toh / <u>bahn</u>-dah fah-voh-<u>ree</u>-tah?*

My favorite movie / book / band is….
>Mi película favorita / libro favorito / banda favorita es…
>>*Mee peh-<u>lee</u>-coo-lah fah-voh-<u>ree</u>-tah / <u>lee</u>-broh fah-voh-<u>ree</u>-toh / <u>bahn</u>-dah fah-voh-<u>ree</u>-tah ehs…*

What is your take on this?
>¿Cuál es tu opinión sobre…?
>>*¿Kwahl ehs too oh-pee-<u>nee-ohn</u> <u>soh</u>-breh…?*

What do you think?
>¿Qué opinas?
>>*¿Keh oh-<u>pee</u>-nahs?*

What are your thoughts on this?
>¿Qué te parece esto?
>>*¿Keh teh pah-<u>reh</u>-ceh <u>ehs</u>-toh?*

Where do you live?
>¿Dónde vives?
>>*¿<u>Dohn</u>-deh <u>vee</u>-vehs?*

Is it a very large city?
>¿Es una ciudad grande?
>>*¿Ehs oo-nah see-oo-<u>dahd</u> <u>grahn</u>-deh?*

What city are you from?
>¿De qué ciudad eres?
>>*¿Deh keh see-oo-<u>dahd</u> <u>eh</u>-rehs?*

Were you born here?
> ¿Naciste aquí?
>> *¿Nah-sees-teh ah-kee?*

I'm looking for temporary work.
> Busco un trabajo temporal.
>> *Boos-coh oon trah-bah-hoh tehm-poh-rahl*

I'm the general manager.
> Soy el gerente general.
>> *Soy ehl heh-rehn-teh heh-neh-rahl*

Do you have a business card?
> ¿Tienes una tarjeta profesional?
>> *¿Tee-eh-nehs oo-nah tahr-heh-tah proh-feh-see-oh-nahl?*

What company do you work for?
> ¿En qué compañía trabajas?
>> *¿En keh cohm-pah-nyee-ah trah-bah-hahs?*

I'm an independent contractor.
> Soy un trabajador independiente.
>> *Soy oon trah-bah-hah-dohr een-deh-pehn-dee-ehn-teh*

Relationships

Let's be on first-name terms.
Tutéame.
Too-teh-ah-meh

I'm glad to be your friend.
Me alegra ser tu amigo/a.
Meh ah-leh-grah ser too ah-mee-goh/ah

You're very likeable.
Me caes bien.
Meh cah-ehs bee-ehn

You're cool.
Eres buena onda.
Eh-rehs boo-eh-nah ohn-dah

I think we're going to get along well.
Creo que vamos a llevarnos bien.
Creh-oh que vah-mohs ah ee-eh-vahr-nohs bee-ehn

Will you go with me?
¿Me acompañas?
¿Meh ah-cohm-pah-nyas?

Would you like to have dinner with me?
¿Quisieras cenar conmigo?
¿Kee-see-eh-rahs ceh-nahr cohn-mee-goh?

I want to invite you to…
Quiero invitarte a…
Kee-eh-roh een-vee-tahr-teh a…

What would you prefer to do now?
¿Qué prefieres hacer ahora?
¿Keh preh-fee-eh-rehs ah-sehr ah-oh-rah?

Where do you want to go tonight?
¿A dónde vamos esta noche?
¿Ah dohn-deh vah-mohs ehs-tah noh-cheh?

I'll wait for you in an hour.
Te espero en una hora.
Teh ehs-peh-roh en oo-nah oh-rah

Where shall I wait for you?

¿Dónde te espero?

¿Dohn-deh teh ehs-peh-roh?

I can pick you up at 6.

Puedo pasar a buscarte a las seis.

Pwe-doh pah-sahr a boos-cahr-teh ah lahs seh-ees

I'll meet you at the hotel.

Te encuentro en el hotel.

Teh ehn-kwehn-troh ehn ehl oh-tehl

You look very pretty.

Te ves muy bonita.

Teh vehs mooy boh-nee-tah

Wow, how handsome!

¡Ay, qué guapo!

¡Ay, keh wah-poh!

I had a nice time with you.

La he pasado muy bien contigo.

Lah eh pah-sah-doh mooy bee-ehn cohn-tee-goh

I'd like to keep in touch with you.

Me gustaría seguir en contacto contigo.

Meh goos-tah-ree-ah seh-geer ehn cohn-tahc-toh cohn-tee-goh

Let's not lose touch, okay?

No perdamos el contacto, ¿eh?

Noh pehr-dah-mosh ehl cohn-tahc-toh, ¿eh?

I'll send you a message when I get to the hotel.

Te mandaré un mensaje cuando llegue al hotel.

Teh mahn-dah-reh oon mehn-sah-heh kwahn-doh ee-eh-gueh al oh-tehl

Give me a call.

Dame una llamada.

Da-meh oo-nah ee-ah-mah-dah

This is my phone number.

Este es mi número de teléfono.

Ehs-teh ehs mee noo-meh-roh deh teh-leh-foh-noh

Leave me a voice message.
Déjame un mensaje de voz.
Deh-hah-meh oon mehn-sah-jeh deh vohss

Do you use social media?
¿Usas alguna red social?
¿Usas al-goo-nah rehd soh-see-ahl?

Would you give me your phone number?
¿Me darías tu número de teléfono?
¿Meh dah-ree-ahs too nuh-meh-ro deh teh-leh-foh-noh?

I'll call you for the next date.
Te llamaré para la próxima cita.
Teh ee-ah-mah-reh pah-rah lah proh-xee-mah see-tah

I can't wait to see you again.
No puedo esperar a verte otra vez.
Noh pwe-doh ehs-peh-rarh ah vehr-teh oh-trah vehs

I'll pay for dinner tonight.
Esta noche yo pagaré la cena.
Ehs-tah noh-cheh yo pah-gah-reh lah ceh-nah

You look amazing.
Te ves increíble.
Teh vehs een-creh-ee-bleh

We can go to my hotel.
Podemos ir a mi hotel.
Poh-deh-mohs eer ah mee oh-tehl

I'll pick you up tonight.
Te recogeré esta noche.
Teh reh-coh-heh-reh ehs-tah noh-cheh

What time does the party start?
¿A qué hora empieza la fiesta?
¿A keh oh-rah em-pee-ehs-ah la fee-ehs-tah?

May I hold your hand?
¿Puedo tomarte de la mano?
¿Pwe-doh toh-mahr-teh deh lah mah-noh?

I'll give you a ride.
Te daré un aventón.

Teh dah-<u>reh</u> oon ah-vehn-<u>tohn</u>

Are you free tonight?

¿Estás libre esta noche?

¿Ehs-<u>tahs</u> <u>lee</u>-breh <u>ehs</u>-tah <u>noh</u>-cheh?

Can I hug you?

¿Puedo darte un abrazo?

¿<u>Pwe</u>-doh <u>dahr</u>-teh oon ah-<u>brah</u>-soh?

Shall we split the bill?

¿Dividimos la cuenta?

¿Dee-vee-<u>dee</u>-mohs lah <u>kwehn</u>-tah?

Being Polite

Thank you	Gracias	*Grah-see-ahs*
You're welcome	De nada	*Deh nah-dah*
No problem	No hay de qué	*Noh I deh keh*
Excuse me (when sorry)	Disculpe	*Dees-cool-peh*
I'm sorry	Lo siento	*Loh see-ehn-toh*
Excuse me (when being polite)	Permiso	*Pehr-mee-soh*
I'm sorry to interrupt	Lamento interrumpir	*Lah-mehn-toh een-teh-room-peer*
That's a shame	Es una lástima	*Ehs oo-nah lahs-tee-mah*
Good luck!	¡Suerte!	*¡Soo-ehr-teh!*
Cheers/Bless you	Salud	*Sah-lood*
Don't worry	No te preocupes	*Noh teh preh-oh-coo-pehs*

Allow me to introduce you to my friend...
Quiero presentarte a mi amigo...
Kee-eh-roh preh-sehn-tahr-teh ah mee ah-mee-goh

I'm sorry for your loss.
Lamento tu pérdida.
Lah-mehn-toh too pehr-dee-dah

How can I help you?
¿Cómo puedo ayudarte?
¿Coh-moh pwe-doh ah-yoo-dahr-teh?

I apologize for being late.
Perdón por la tardanza.
Pehr-dohn pohr lah tahr-dahn-sah

That was my fault.
Fue mi culpa.
Foo-eh mee cool-pah

It won't happen again.

No volverá a suceder.

Noh vohl-veh-<u>rah</u> ah soo-seh-<u>dehr</u>

Having a Conversation

It's been a long time.
Ha pasado mucho tiempo.
Ah pah-sah-doh moo-choh tee-ehm-poh

Home, sweet home.
Hogar, dulce hogar.
Oh-gahr, dool-ceh oh-gahr

I'm going to have to have a think about that.
Tengo que pensarlo.
Tehn-goh keh pehn-sahr-loh

Let me think about it.
Déjame pensarlo.
Deh-hah-meh pehn-sahr-loh

Give me a moment.
Dame un momento.
Dah-meh oon moh-mehn-toh

Now that's a good question.
Esa es una buena pregunta.
Eh-sah ehs oo-nah boo-eh-nah preh-goon-tah

I'm not really sure.
No estoy muy seguro.
Noh ehs-toy mooy seh-goo-roh

I don't have a clue.
No tengo ni idea.
Noh tehn-goh nee ee-deh-ah

Who knows.
Quién sabe.
Kee-ehn sah-beh

I don't know for sure.
No lo sé con seguridad.
Noh loh seh cohn seh-goo-ree-dahd

How interesting!
¡Qué interesante!
¡Keh een-teh-reh-sahn-teh!

Fantastic!

¡Fantástico!

¡Fahn-tahs-tee-coh!

This is fascinating.

Me fascina esto.

Meh fah-see-nah ehs-toh

How boring!

¡Qué aburrido!

¡Keh ah-boo-ree-doh!

You don't say.

No me digas.

Noh meh dee-gahs

That's how it is.

Así es.

Ah-see ehs

Isn't that right?

¿No es cierto?

¿Noh ehs see-ehr-toh?

Seriously?

¿En serio?

¿Ehn seh-ree-oh?

Really?

¿De veras?

¿Deh veh-rahs?

In fact...

De hecho...

Deh eh-choh...

By the way...

A propósito...

Ah proh-poh-see-toh...

You are right.

Tienes razón.

Tee-eh-nehs rah-sohn

Certainly.

Claro que sí.

Clah-roh keh see

Absolutely not.
En absoluto.
Ehn ahb-soh-loo-toh

It seems fine to me.
Me parece muy bien.
Meh pah-reh-ceh mooy bee-ehn

Do tell all.
Cuéntamelo todo.
Kwehn-tah-meh-loh toh-doh

I want to know everything.
Lo quiero saber todo.
Loh kee-eh-roh sah-behr toh-doh

I think you're mistaken.
Creo que te equivocas.
Creh-oh keh teh eh-kee-voh-cahs

How funny!
¡Qué gracioso!
¡Keh grah-see-oh-soh!

You're exaggerating!
Estás exagerando.
Ehs-tahs ehx-sah-heh-rahn-doh

Please be quiet.
Por favor, haz silencio.
Pohr fah-vohr, ahs see-lehn-see-oh

Don't interrupt me while I'm talking.
No me interrumpas cuando estoy hablando.
Noh meh een-teh-room-pahs kwahn-doh ehs-toy ah-blahn-doh

Don't be rude.
No seas grosero.
Noh seh-ahs groh-seh-roh

Could you lower your voice?
¿Podrías bajar la voz?
¿Poh-dree-ahs bah-hahr lah vohs?

Don't yell at me.
> No me grites.
>> *Noh meh gree-tehs*

When did you arrive?
> ¿Cuándo llegaste?
>> *¿Kwahn-doh yeh-gahs-teh?*

It was a pleasant flight.
> Fue un vuelo agradable.
>> *Foo-eh oon bweh-loh ah-grah-dah-bleh*

I have jetlag, I need to lie down.
> Tengo jetlag, necesito recostarme.
>> *Tehn-goh jetlag, neh-seh-see-toh reh-cohs-tahr-meh*

Do you have a lighter?
> ¿Tienes un encendedor?
>> *¿Tee-eh-nehs oon ehn-sehn-deh-dohr?*

I'll be working late tonight.
> Trabajaré hasta tarde esta noche.
>> *Trah-bah-hah-reh ahs-tah tahr-deh ehs-tah noh-cheh*

How was your trip?
> ¿Cómo estuvo el viaje?
>> *¿Coh-moh ehs-too-voh ehl vee-ah-heh?*

Tourism

There is a free concert in the central park.
Hay un concierto gratuito en el parque central.
I oon cohn-see-ehr-toh grah-too-ee-toh ehn ehl par-keh cehn-trahl

Are there any seats available?
¿Aún hay asientos disponibles?
¿Ah-oon i ah-see-en-tohs dees-poh-nee-blehs?

Are there movie theaters with movies in English?
¿Hay cines con películas en inglés?
¿I cee-nehs cohn peh-lee-coo-lahs ehn een-glehs?

What movies are they showing now?
¿Qué películas dan ahora?
¿Keh peh-lee-coo-lahs dahn ah-oh-rah?

Can you get me a ticket?
¿Puedes conseguirme una entrada?
¿Pwe-dehs cohn-seh-geer-meh oo-na ehn-trah-dah?

Is it dubbed or does it have subtitles?
¿Es doblada o tiene subtítulos?
¿Ehs doh-blah-dah oh tee-eh-neh soob-tee-too-lohs?

We would like two tickets to the movie...
Quisiéramos dos entradas para la película...
Kee-see-eh-rah-mohs dohs ehn-trah-dahs pah-rah lah peh-lee-coo-la ....

Are there any tourist attractions for children?
¿Hay alguna atracción turística para niños?
¿I ahl-goo-nah ah-trahk-see-ohn too-rees-tee-cah pah-rah nee-nyohs?

Where do local people go for fun?
¿A dónde va la gente de la zona para divertirse?
¿Ah dohn-deh vah lah hehn-teh deh lah soh-nah pah-rah dee-vehr-teer-seh?

Is there a mall nearby?
¿Hay una plaza comercial cerca?

41

¿I oo-nah plah-zah coh-mehr-ceeahl cehr-cah?

What kinds of activities are there for teens?

¿Qué actividades hay para adolescentes?

¿Keh ack-tee-bee-dah-dehs i pah-rah ah-doh-leh-sehn-tehs?

Are there amusement parks?

¿Hay parques de diversiones?

¿I pahr-kehs deh dee-vehr-seeoh-nehs?

Is there a national park nearby?

¿Hay un parque nacional cerca de aquí?

¿I oon pahr-keh nah-cee-oh-nahl cer-cah deh ah-kee?

Are there tours to see places of historical interest?

¿Hay excursiones para ver lugares de interés histórico?

¿I ehx-coor-seeoh-nehs pah-rah vehr loo-gah-res deh een-teh-rehs ees-toh-ree-coh?

Are there museums here?

¿Hay museos aquí?

¿I moo-seh-ohs ah-kee?

What is the best tour for families?

¿Cuál es la mejor excursión para una familia?

¿Cooahl ehs lah meh-hor ehx-coor-seeohn pah-rah oo-nah fah-mee-leeah?

Can you take our picture, please?

¿Puedes tomarnos una foto, por favor?

¿Pwe-dehs toh-mahr-nohs oo-nah foh-toh, porh fah-vohr?

Where is the zoo?

¿Dónde se encuentra el zoológico?

¿Dohn-deh seh ehn-cooehn-trah ehl zoh-loh-hee-coh?

What kind of animal is that?

¿Qué tipo de animal es?

¿Keh tee-poh deh ah-nee-mahl ehs?

Is that animal dangerous?

¿Es un animal peligroso?

¿Ehs oon ah-nee-mahl pehlee-groh-soh?

Are kids allowed?

¿Se admiten niños?
¿Seh ahd-mee-tehn nee-nyohs?

Can I smoke in this area?
¿Puedo fumar aquí?
¿Pwe-doh foo-mahr ah-kee?

Where can I find an internet café?
¿Dónde hay un cyber café?
¿Dohn-deh I oon cee-behr cah-feh?

The keyboard isn't working correctly.
El teclado no funciona.
Ehl the-clah-doh noh foon-ceeoh-nah

Where can I get a map of the area?
¿Dónde consigo un mapa de la zona?
¿Dohn-deh cohn-see-goh oon mah-pah deh lah zoh-nah?

Are there any hiking trails?
¿Hay rutas de excursionismo?
¿I roo-tahs deh ehx-coor-seeoh-nees-moh?

Are there any trails for mountain biking?
¿Hay rutas de ciclismo de montaña?
¿I roo-tahs deh cee-clees-moh deh mohn-tah-nyah?

Which route is the easiest?
¿Cuál es la ruta más fácil?
¿Cooalh ehs lah roo-tah mahs fah-ceel?

Is this track well marked?
¿Está bien marcada la ruta?
¿Ehs-tah bee-ehn mahr-cah-dah lah roo-tah?

Is there a cabin to spend the night?
¿Hay una cabaña donde pasar la noche?
¿I oo-nah cah-bah-nyah dohn-deh pah-sahr lah noh-cheh?

We're lost.
Nos perdimos.
Nohs per-dee-mohs

What is that building?
¿Qué es ese edificio?
¿Keh ehs eh-seh eh-dee-fee-see-oh?

Can I hire a guide?

¿Se puede contratar un guía?

¿Seh pwe-deh cohn-trah-tahr oon guee-ah?

Do you have a brochure?

¿Hay folletos disponibles?

¿I foh-iee-tohs dees-poh-nee-bles?

Can I camp here?

¿Se puede acampar aquí?

¿Seh pweh-deh ah-cahm-pahr ah-kee?

How much is it for a tent?

¿Cuánto es por tienda?

¿Kwahn-toh ehs pohr tee-ehn-dah?

Do you have electricity?

¿Tiene electricidad?

¿Tee-eh-neh ehl-ehc-tree-cee-dahd?

Cultural

Where is the National Art Museum?
¿Dónde está el Museo Nacional de Arte?
¿Dohn-deh ehs-tah ehl moo-seh-oh nah-see-oh-nahl deh ahr-teh?

Are there organized tours of the museum?
¿Hay excursiones organizadas para el museo?
¿I ehx-coor-see-oh-nehs ohr-ga-nee-zah-dahs pah-rah ehl moo-seh-oh?

How much is the entrance fee?
¿Cuánto cuesta la entrada?
¿Kwahn-toh kwehs-tah lah ehn-trah-dah?

Do you offer child discounts?
¿Ofrecen descuentos para niños?
¿Oh-freh-cehn dehs-kwehn-tohs pah-rah nee-nyos?

What are the museum's opening hours?
¿Cuáles son las horas del museo?
¿Kwah-lehs son lahs oh-rahs dehl moo-seh-oh?

Is it open every day?
¿Está abierto todos los días?
¿Ehs-tah ah-bee-ehr-toh toh-dohs lohs dee-ahs?

Where is the nearest entrance/exit?
¿Dónde está la entrada/salida más cercana?
¿Dohn-deh ehs-tah lah ehn-trah-dah/sah-lee-dah mahs cehr-cah-nah?

Where is the ... collection?
¿Dónde está la colección de...?
¿Dohn-deh ehs-tah lah coh-lehk-see-ohn deh...?

Do you have a tour in English?
¿Tienen un tour en inglés?
¿Tee-eh-nehn un tour en een-glehs?

Is there a recorded tour?
¿Tienen audioguía?
¿Tee-eh-nehn aoo-dee-oh-ghee-ah?

My headphones don't work.

Mis audífonos no funcionan.

Mees ah-oo-dee-foh-nohs noh foon-see-oh-nahn

Is there a special exhibit on now?

¿Hay alguna exhibición especial ahora?

¿I ahl-goo-nah ehx-see-bee-see-ohn ehs-peh-see-ahl ah-oh-rah?

Where is the gift shop?

¿Dónde está la tienda de regalos?

¿Dohn-deh ehs-tah la tee-ehn-dah de reh-gah-lohs?

I'd like to buy a copy of …

Quisiera comprar una reproducción de…

Kee-see-eh-rah cohm-prahr una reh-proh-dook-see-ohn deh…

Is there a safe place where I can leave my backpack?

¿Hay un lugar seguro donde pueda dejar la mochila?

¿I oon loo-gahr seh-goo-roh dohn-deh pwe-dah deh-jahr lah moh-chee-lah?

Is there a place where I could pray?

¿Hay un lugar donde pueda rezar?

¿I un loo-gahr dohn-deh pwe-dah reh-zahr?

When are the church services?

¿A qué hora son las misas?

¿A kee oh-rah son lahs mee-sahs?

How long does the church service last?

¿Cuánto dura la misa?

¿Kwahn-toh doo-rah la mee-sah?

What is the appropriate dress code?

¿Cuál es el código de vestimenta apropiado?

¿Kwahl ehs el coh-dee-goh deh vehs-tee-mehn-tah ah-proh-pee-ah-doh?

Where is the nearest Catholic church?

¿Dónde se encuentra la iglesia católica más cercana?

¿Dohn-deh seh ehn-kwehn-trah lah ee-gleh-see-ah cah-toh-lee-cah mahs cehr-cah-nah?

Is there a mosque?

¿Hay una mezquita?
> *¿I una mehs-<u>kee</u>-tah?*

Who is getting married?

¿Quién se casa?
> *¿Kee-ehn seh <u>cah</u>-sah?*

What is the charge for marrying us?

¿Cuál es el costo por casarnos?
> *¿Kwahl ehs el <u>cohs</u>-toh pohr cah-<u>sahr</u>-nos?*

Where do we get a marriage license?

¿Dónde se consiguen las licencias de matrimonio?
> *¿<u>Dohn</u>-deh seh cohn-<u>see</u>-gehn las lee-<u>cehn</u>-cee-ahs deh mah-tree-<u>moh</u>-nyo?*

Please gather here to pray.

Por favor, acérquense para rezar.
> *Porh fah-<u>vohr</u>, ah-<u>serh</u>-ken-seh <u>pah</u>-rah reh-<u>zahr</u>*

Are mobile phones allowed in this building?

¿Se pueden usar teléfonos móviles en este edificio?
> *¿Seh <u>pwe</u>-dehn oo-<u>sahr</u> teh-<u>leh</u>-foh-nohs <u>moh</u>-bee-lehs ehn <u>ehs</u>-teh eh-dee-<u>fee</u>-see-oh?*

Do you accept donations?

¿Se aceptan limosnas?
> *¿Seh ah-<u>cehp</u>-tahn lee-<u>mohs</u>-nahs?*

What book should I be reading from?

¿De qué libro debería leer?
> *¿Deh keh <u>lee</u>-broh deh-beh-<u>ree</u>-ah leh-<u>ehr</u>?*

Nightlife

Is there a pub/bar around here?

¿Hay algún bar por aquí?

¿I ahl-goon bahr pohr ah-kee?

Can you recommend me a place to dance?

¿Me podrías recomendar un lugar para bailar?

¿Meh poh-dree-ahs reh-coh-mehn-dahr oon loo-gahr pah-rah bye-lahr?

Can you recommend me something fun to do tonight?

¿Me podrías recomendar algo divertido para hacer esta noche?

¿Meh poh-dree-ahs reh-coh-men-dahr ahl-goh dee-ver-tee-doh pah-rah hah-cer ehs-tah noh-che?

Where do young people go for fun?

¿A dónde va la gente joven para divertirse?

¿Ah dohn-deh vah lah hehn-teh hoh-ven pah-rah dee-ver-teer-seh?

I want to go to a dance nightclub.

Quiero ir a una discoteca.

Kee-eh-roh eer ah oo-nah dees-coh-teh-cah

I love this place.

Me encanta este lugar.

Meh ehn-cahn-tah ehs-teh loo-gahr

I don't like this place.

No me gusta este lugar.

Noh meh goos-tah ehs-teh loo-gahr

Let's go somewhere else.

Vayamos a otro lugar.

Bah-ee-ah-mohs ah oh-troh loo-gahr

What are you drinking?

¿Qué tomas?

¿Keh toh-mahs?

I'll buy you a drink.

Te invito a un trago.

Teh een-vee-toh ah oon trah-goh

Would you like to dance with me?

¿Bailarías conmigo?

¿Bye-lah-<u>ree</u>-ahs cohn-<u>mee</u>-goh?

Money

Where can I change money?
¿Dónde puedo cambiar dinero?
¿Dohn-deh pwe-doh cahm-bee-ahr dee-neh-roh?

I want to change dollars for pesos.
Quiero cambiar dólares por pesos.
Kee-eh-roh cahm-bee-ahr doh-lah-rehs por peh-sohs.

What's the dollar rate today?
¿A cuánto está el dólar hoy?
¿A kwahn-toh ehs-tah el doh-lahr oi?

I need small change.
Necesito cambio.
Neh-seh-see-toh cahm-bee-oh

I prefer larger bills.
Prefiero billetes de mayor valor.
Preh-fee-eh-roh bee-eh-tehs de mah-ee-ohr vah-lohr

How much do you wish to change?
¿Cuánto deseas cambiar?
¿Kwahn-toh deh-seh-ahs cahm-bee-ahr?

I want to change 200 dollars.
Quiero cambiar doscientos dólares.
Kee-eh-roh cahm-bee-ahr dohs-see-ehn-tohs doh-lah-rehs

What time does the bank open/close?
¿A qué hora abre/cierra el banco?
¿Ah keh oh-rah ah-breh/see-eh-rah el bahn-coh?

Do you accept credit cards?
¿Aceptan tarjeta de crédito?
¿Ah-cehp-tahn tahr-jeh-tah de creh-dee-toh?

May I pay with traveler's checks?
¿Puedo pagar con cheques de viajero?
¿Pwe-doh pah-gahr cohn cheh-kehs deh vee-ah-jeh-roh?

Where is the ATM?
¿Dónde está el cajero automático?
¿Dohn-deh ehs-tah el cah-jeh-roh ah-oo-toh-mah-tee-coh?

The machine ate my card.

La máquina me tragó la tarjeta.

Lah <u>mah</u>-kee-nah meh trah-<u>goh</u> lah tahr-<u>heh</u>-tah

When will you be able to get my card out?

¿Cuándo van a poder sacar mi tarjeta?

¿<u>Kwahn</u>-doh vahn ah poh-<u>dehr</u> sah-<u>cahr</u> mee tahr-<u>jeh</u>-tah?

Shopping

I'd like to see something...
Quiero ver algo...
Kee-eh-roh vehr ahl-goh...

I'm looking for a souvenir.
Busco un recuerdo.
Boos-coh oon reh-kwehr-doh

It's for my wife.
Es para mi esposa.
Ehs pah-rah mee ehs-poh-sah

I'm just looking.
Sólo estoy mirando.
Soh-loh ehs-toy mee-rahn-doh

It's a bit large/small.
Es un poco grande/pequeño.
Ehs oon poh-coh grahn-deh/peh-keh-nyo

What is it made of?
¿De qué es?
¿Deh keh ehs?

Is this real leather?
¿Es cuero verdadero?
¿Ehs kweh-roh vehr-dah-deh-roh?

Is this synthetic?
¿Es sintético?
¿Ehs seen-teh-tee-coh?

Is this pure cotton?
¿Es algodón puro?
¿Ehs ahl-goh-dohn poo-roh?

Is this hypoallergenic?
¿Es hipoalergénico?
¿Ehs ee-poh-ah-lehr-geh-nee-coh?

Where do these products come from?
¿De dónde vienen estos productos?
¿Deh don-deh vee-eh-nehn ehs-tohs proh-dooc-tohs?

Do you have this shirt in a smaller size?

¿Tienes esta camisa en una talla más pequeña?

¿Tee-eh-neh ehs-tah cah-mee-sah ehn oo-nah tie-yah mahs peh-keh-nya?

I need a size S/M/L.

Necesito talla S/M/L.

Neh-seh-see-toh tie-yah S/M/L.

I'd like to try this.

Me gustaría probar esto.

Meh goos-tah-ree-ah proh-bahr ehs-toh.

Does this suit me?

¿Me queda bien?

¿Meh keh-dah bee-ehn?

How much is it?

¿Cuánto cuesta esto?

¿Kwahn-toh kwehs-tah ehs-toh?

I'll take it.

Me lo llevo.

Meh loh ee-eh-voh.

Can I have a refund?

¿Puedo obtener un reembolso?

¿Pwe-doh ohb-teh-nehr oon rehm-bohl-soh?

Can I exchange this for another item?

¿Puedo cambiarlo por otro artículo?

¿Pwe-doh cahm-bee-ahr-loh pohr oh-troh ahr-tee-coo-loh?

Can I pay in dollars?

¿Puedo pagar en dólares?

¿Pwe-doh pah-gahr ehn doh-lah-rehs?

Do you have an online shop?

¿Tienen una tienda online?

¿Tee-eh-nehn oo-nah tee-ehn-dah online?

Is this your only shop in town?

¿Es su única tienda en la ciudad?

¿Ehs soo oo-nee-cah tee-ehn-dah ehn lah seeh-oo-dahd?

Is it possible to finance these products?

¿Es posible financiar estos productos?
¿Ehs po-see-bleh fee-nahn-see-ahr ehs-tohs proh-dooc-tohs?

Is there tax free shopping?
¿Existen comercios libres de impuestos?
¿Ex-ees-tehn coh-mehr-see-ohs lee-brehs deh eem-pwehs-toh?

What time do the shops open in this area?
¿A qué hora abren los comercios en esta zona?
¿A keh oh-rah ah-brehn lohs coh-mehr-see-ohs ehn ehs-tah zoh-nah?

May I try this on?
¿Me lo puedo probar?
¿Meh loh pwe-doh proh-bahr?

Where should I sign?
¿Dónde firmo?
¿Don-deh feer-moh?

Can we haggle over the price?
¿Podemos negociar el precio?
¿Poh-deh-mohs neh-goh-see-ahr ehl preh-see-oh?

Can you wrap that as a gift?
¿Podrías envolverlo para regalo?
¿Poh-dree-ahs ehn-vohl-vehr-loh pah-rah reh-gah-loh?

Can you send it to my hotel?
¿Podrías enviarlo a mi hotel?
¿Poh-dree-ahs ehn-vee-ahr-loh ah mee oh-tehl?

Your commission rate is too high.
La comisión es muy alta.
Lah coh-mee-see-ohn ehs mooy ahl-tah.

Where is the cashier?
¿Dónde está la caja?
¿Dohn-deh eh-stah lah cah-hah?

How much is this item with tax?
¿Cuánto cuesta esto con impuesto incluído?
¿Kwahn-toh kwehs-tah ehs-toh cohn eem-pwehs-toh een-cloo-ee-doh?

Can I have a bag for that?
¿Me podrías dar una bolsa?

¿Meh poh-dree-ahs dahr oo-nah bohl-sah?

Common Vocabulary

Bookstore	Librería	*Lee-breh-<u>ree</u>-ah*
Department store	Almacén	*Ahl-mah-<u>sehn</u>*
Clothing store	Tienda de ropa	*<u>Tee-ehn</u>-dah deh <u>roh</u>-pah*
Grocery store	Tienda de comestibles	*<u>Tee-ehn</u>-dah deh coh-mehs-tee-blehs*
Supermarket	Supermercado	*Soo-pehr-mehr-cah-doh*
Shoe store	Zapatería	*Zah-pah-teh-<u>ree</u>-ah*
Gift shop	Tienda de regalos	*<u>Tee-ehn</u>-dah deh reh-<u>gah</u>-lohs*
Florist	Florería	*Floh-reh-<u>ree</u>-ah*
Jewelry	Joyería	*Ho-yeh-<u>ree</u>-ah*
News stand	Puesto de periódicos	*<u>Pwehs</u>-toh deh peh-<u>ree-oh</u>-dee-cohs*
Toy store	Juguetería	*Hooh-gueh-teh-<u>ree</u>-ah*
T-shirt	Playera/Camiseta	*Plah-<u>yeh</u>-rah/Cah-mee-<u>seh</u>-tah*
Shirt	Camisa	*Cah-<u>mee</u>-sah*
Blouse	Blusa	*<u>Blooh</u>-sah*
Blazer	Americana	*Ah-meh-ree-<u>cah</u>-nah*
Bodysuit	Body	*Body*
Sweatshirt	Sudadera	*Soo-dah-<u>deh</u>-rah*
Sweater	Jersey	*Jersey*
Pants	Pantalón	*Pahn-tah-<u>lohn</u>*
Trousers	Pantalón	*Pahn-tah-<u>lohn</u>*
Jeans	Pantalón vaquero	*Pahn-tah-<u>lohn</u> vah-<u>keh</u>-roh*
Shorts	Pantalón corto/Short	*Pahn-tah-<u>lohn</u> cohr-toh/Short*
Joggers	Joggers	*Joggers*

Sweat pants/ Track pants	Pantalón de jogging	*Pahn-tah-lohn deh jogging*
Dress	Vestido	*Vehs-tee-doh*
Skirt	Falda	*Fahl-dah*
Underwear	Ropa interior	*Roh-pah een-teh-ree-ohr*
Bra	Sostén	*Sohs-tehn*
Panties	Braga	*Brah-gah*
Briefs/Boxers	Calzoncillos	*Cahl-zon-see-yohs*
Socks	Calcetines	*Cahl-ceh-tee-nehs*
Pyjamas	Pijama	*Pee-yah-mah*
Bathing suit/Swimsuit	Traje de baño	*Trah-jeh deh bah-nyo*
Trunks	Bañador	*Bah-nya-dohr*
Leggings	Mallas	*Mah-yahs*
Coat	Abrigo	*Ah-bree-goh*
Jacket	Chaqueta	*Cha-keh-tah*
Sneakers	Zapatillas deportivas	*Zah-pah-tee-yahs deh-pohr-tee-vahs*
Cap	Gorra	*Goh-rah*
Hat/Snow hat	Gorro	*Goh-roh*
Belt	Cinturón	*Seen-too-ron*
Necklace	Collar	*Coh-yahr*
Bracelet	Pulsera	*Pool-seh-rah*
Watch	Reloj	*Reh-lohj*
Earrings	Aretes	*Ah-reh-tehs*
Ring	Anillo	*Ah-nee-yoh*
Gloves	Guantes	*Gwahn-tehs*
Mittens	Manoplas	*Mah-noh-plahs*
Scarf	Bufanda	*Boo-fahn-dah*
Sunglasses	Gafas de sol	*Gah-fahs deh sohl*

Bargaining

How much for this souvenir?

¿Cuánto cuesta este recuerdo?

¿Kwahn-toh kwehs-tah ehs-teh reh-kwehr-doh?

What's your best price?

¿Cuál es tu mejor precio?

¿Kwahl ehs too meh-hohr preh-see-oh?

Could you go a bit lower?

¿Podrías bajar un poco el precio?

¿Poh-dree-ahs bah-hahr oon poh-coh ehl preh-see-oh?

How much is it if I take 3?

¿Cuánto cuesta si me llevo 3?

¿Kwahn-toh kwehs-tah see meh yeh-voh trehs?

Would you give me a discount?

¿Me harías un descuento?

¿Meh ah-ree-ahs oon dehs-kwehn-toh?

I don't think it's that cheap.

No me parece tan barato.

Noh meh pah-reh-seh tahn bah-rah-toh

It's too expensive.

Es muy caro.

Ehs mooy cah-roh

I'll give you 15 pesos.

Te doy 15 pesos.

The dohy keen-seh peh-sohs

Would you take 10?

¿Aceptarías 10?

¿Ah-sehp-tah-ree-ahs dee-ehs?

This is as high as I go.

Es lo máximo que estoy dispuesto a pagar.

Ehs loh mahx-see-moh keh ehs-toy dees-pwehs-toh ah pah-gahr

Deal.

Trato.

Trah-toh

That's okay, I'm not interested then.

Está bien, no me interesa entonces.

Ehs-tah bee-ehn, noh meh een-teh-reh-sah ehn-tohn-sehs

Exercise Related

What sports do you usually play?

¿Qué deportes practicas habitualmente?

¿Keh deh-pohr-tehs prahc-tee-cahs ah-bee-too-ahl-mehn-teh?

Do you want to play basketball with me?

¿Quieres jugar conmigo al básket?

¿Kee-eh-rehs hooh-gahr cohn-mee-goh al basket?

I play tennis every week.

Juego al tenis todas las semanas.

Hooh-eh-goh ahl tenis toh-dahs lahs seh-mah-nahs

Is there a tennis court close by?

¿Hay una cancha de tenis cerca?

¿I oo-nah cahn-chah de tenis sehr-cah?

I ride my bike on the weekends.

Ando en bicicleta los fines de semana.

Ahn-doh en bee-see-cleh-tah los fee-nehs de seh-mah-nah

I'm going to the gym.

Voy al gimnasio.

Voy al geem-nah-see-oh.

How many days do you work out in a week?

¿Cuántas veces a la semana haces ejercicio?

¿Kwahn-tahs beh-sehs ah lah seh-mah-nah ah-sehs eh-hair-see-see-oh?

What muscles will you work on today?

¿Qué músculos trabajarás hoy?

¿Keh moos-coo-lohs trah-bah-hah-rahs oi?

How many sets do you have left?

¿Cuántas series te quedan?

¿Kwahn-tahs seh-ree-ehs te keh-dahn?

I am training for a (running, swimming, bicycle, etc.) competition.

Estoy entrenando para una competencia de (carrera, natación, ciclismo).

Ehs-toy ehn-treh-nahn-doh pah-rah oo-nah cohm-peh-tehn-see-ah de (cah-reh-rah, nah-tah-see-ohn, see-clees-moh)

Can you spot me? I'm going to try for 6-8 reps.

¿Me echas una mano? Voy a tratar de hacer 6-8 repeticiones.

¿Me eh-chahs oo-nah mah-noh? Voy ah trah-tahr de ah-sehr 6-8 (seh-ees oh-cho) reh-peh-tee-see-oh-nehs

Today is arms and legs day.

Hoy me toca entrenar brazos y piernas.

Oi meh toh-cah ehn-treh-nahr brah-sohs ee pee-ehr-nahs

Tomorrow is biceps and quadriceps day.

Mañana me toca hacer bíceps y cuádriceps.

Mah-nya-nah meh toh-cah ah-sehr bee-sehps ee kwah-dree-sehps

Can you recommend me a routine?

¿Me puedes recomendar una rutina?

¿Me pwe-dehs reh-coh-mehn-dahr oo-nah roo-tee-nah?

I want to lose weight and tone up my abs.

Quiero perder peso y tonificar el abdomen.

Kee-eh-roh pehr-dehr peh-soh ee toh-nee-fee-cahr ehl ahb-doh-mehn

Are you using this machine?

¿Estás usando este aparato?

¿Ehs-tahs oo-sahn-doh ehs-teh ah-pah-rah-to?

All members have access to the showers and changing rooms.

Todos los miembros tienen acceso a las duchas y vestidores.

Toh-dohs lohs mee-ehm-brohs tee-eh-nehn ahc-seh-soh ah lahs doo-chahs ee vehs-tee-doh-rehs

The yoga studio opens at 7:00 am.

La sala de yoga abre a las 7:00 de la mañana.

Lah sah-lah deh yoga ah-breh ah lahs see-eh-teh deh lah mah-nya-nah

Where can I go for a run?

¿Por dónde puedo correr?

¿Pohr dohn-deh pwe-doh coh-rehr?

How long is this circuit?

¿Cuántas millas tiene este circuito?

¿Kwahn-tahs mee-yahs tee-eh-neh ehs-teh seer-quee-toh?

Where is a running track?

¿Dónde hay una pista de atletismo?

¿Dohn-deh I oo-nah pees-tah deh ah-tleh-tees-moh?

Do you have memberships for tourists?

¿Tienen membresías para turistas?

¿Tee-eh-nehn mehm-breh-see-ahs pah-rah too-rees-tahs?

Is there a time limit on working out here?

¿Hay un límite de tiempo para entrenar aquí?

¿I oon lee-mee-teh deh tee-ehm-poh pah-rah ehn-treh-nahr ah-kee?

Do you sell protein shakes?

¿Venden batidos de proteína?

¿Vehn-dehn bah-tee-dohs deh proh-teh-ee-nah?

I need to buy some equipment.

Necesito comprar equipamiento.

Neh-seh-see-toh cohm-prahr eh-kee-pah-mee-ehn-toh

On your mark, get set, go!

En sus marcas, listos, ¡ya!

Ehn soos mahr-cahs, lees-tohs, ¡yah!

Timeout.

Tiempo muerto.

Tee-ehm-poh mwehr-toh

Shall we go golfing?

¿Vamos a jugar al golf?

¿Vah-mohs a hooh-gahr ahl golf?

Where are the golf carts?

¿Dónde están los carritos de golf?

¿Dohn-deh ehs-tahn lohs cah-ree-tohs deh golf?

Do you have your own clubs?

¿Tienes palos de golf?

¿Tee-eh-nehs pah-lohs deh golf?

Soccer

We won!

¡Ganamos!

¡Gah-nah-mohs!

Let's go! You can do it!

¡Vamos! ¡Tú puedes!

¡Vah-mohs! ¡Too pwe-dehs!

Goal!

¡Gol!

¡Gol!

Lionel Messi is Barcelona's top scorer.

Lionel Messi es el goleador de Barcelona.

Lionel Messi ehs ehl goh-leh-ah-dohr deh Barcelona.

The Real Madrid striker scored a goal to tie the game.

El delantero de Real Madrid metió un gol para empatar el juego.

Ehl deh-lahn-teh-roh deh Real Madrid meh-tee-oh oon gol pah-rah ehm-pah-tahr ehl hooh-eh-goh

The subs are on the bench.

Los suplentes están en el banco.

Lohs soo-plehn-tehs ehs-tahn ehn ehl bahn-coh

The striker was given a yellow card for committing a foul.

Al delantero le mostraron la tarjeta amarilla por cometer una falta.

Ahl deh-lahn-teh-roh leh mohs-trah-rohn lah tahr-jeh-tah ah-mah-ree-yah pohr coh-meh-tehr uh-nah fahl-tah

This weekend is the derby between the two best teams.

Este fin de semana es el clásico entre los dos mejores equipos

Ehs-teh feen deh seh-mah-nah ehs ehl clah-see-coh ehn-treh lohs dohs meh-joh-rehs eh-kee-pohs

There are five minutes left until kick-off.

Faltan cinco minutos para el saque inicial del partido.

Fahl-tahn seen-coh mee-noo-tohs pah-rah ehl sah-keh ee-nee-see-ahl dehl pahr-tee-doh

The referee signaled a corner kick.

El árbitro señaló un tiro de esquina.

Ehl ahr-bee-troh seh-nya-loh un tee-roh deh ehs-kee-nah

Colombia won the match against Costa Rica.

Colombia ganó el partido contra Costa Rica.

Colombia gah-noh ehl pahr-tee-doh cohn-trah Costa Rica

Argentina's goalkeeper is the best in South America.

El arquero de Argentina es el mejor de Sudamérica.

Ehl ahr-keh-roh deh Argentina ehs ehl meh-johr deh soo-dah-meh-ree-cah

The game ended in a tie.

El partido quedó en empate.

Ehl pahr-tee-doh keh-doh ehn ehm-pah-teh

The players wait for half-time to rest.

Los jugadores esperan el medio tiempo para descansar.

Lohs hooh-gah-doh-rehs ehs-peh-rahn ehl meh-dee-oh tee-ehm-poh pah-rah dehs-cahn-sahr

Where can we watch the game?

¿Dónde podemos ver el partido?

¿Dohn-deh poh-deh-mohs vehr ehl pahr-tee-doh?

Which team do you think will win?

¿Qué equipo crees que va a ganar?

¿Keh eh-kee-poh creh-ehs keh vah a gah-nahr?

I'm a . . . fan.

Soy aficionado del equipo...

Soh-y ah-fee-see-oh-nah-doh dehl eh-kee-poh...

That was a bad call by the ref.

Fue una mala decisión del árbitro.

Foo-eh oo-nah mah-lah deh-see-seeohn dehl ahr-bee-troh

At the Beach

Which is the best beach for surfing?

¿Cuál es la mejor playa para surfear?

¿Kwahl ehs lah meh-johr plah-yah pah-rah soor-feh-ahr?

Where is the nearest beach?

¿Dónde está la playa más cercana?

¿Dohn-deh ehs-tah lah plah-yah mahs sehr-cah-nah?

Are there restricted/forbidden areas?

¿Hay áreas restringidas/prohibidas?

¿I ah-reh-ahs rehs-treen-hee-dahs/proh-ee-bee-dahs?

Where can I go scuba diving?

¿Dónde se puede bucear?

¿Dohn-deh se pwe-deh boo-seh-ahr?

Is it safe to swim here?

¿Es seguro nadar aquí?

¿Ehs seh-goo-roh nah-dahr ah-kee?

You can dive here.

Se puede echar clavados.

Seh pwe-deh eh-charh clah-vah-dohs.

Is the water clean?

¿El agua está limpia?

¿Ehl ah-wa ehs-tah leem-pee-ah?

Is there a lifeguard on duty?

¿Hay un salvavidas de servicio?

¿I oon sahl-vah-vee-dahs deh sehr-vee-see-oh?

Where can I rent a beach umbrella?

¿Dónde puedo alquilar una sombrilla?

¿Dohn-deh pwe-doh ahl-kee-lahr oo-nah sohm-bree-yah?

Are there toilets on the beach?

¿Hay sanitarios en la playa?

¿I sah-nee-tah-ree-ohs ehn lah plah-yah?

How much does it cost to rent the jet skis?

¿Cuánto cuesta alquilar los jet esquí?

¿Kwahn-toh kwehs-tah ahl-kee-lahr lohs jet es-kee?

Can you put suncream on my back?

¿Me puedes poner crema en la espalda?

¿Meh pwe-dehs poh-nehr creh-mah ehn lah ehs-pahl-dah?

I've been stung by a jellyfish!

¡Me ha picado una medusa!

¡Meh ha pee-cah-doh oo-nah meh-doo-sah!

Where can I buy something to drink?

¿Dónde puedo comprar algo para beber?

¿Dohn-deh pwe-doh cohm-prahr ahl-goh pah-rah beh-behr?

Let's make sandcastles.

Hagamos castillos de arena.

Ah-gah-mohs cahs-tee-yohs deh ah-reh-nah

I want to buy a bathing suit.

Quiero comprarme un traje de baño.

Kee-eh-roh cohm-prahr-meh oon trah-jeh deh bah-nyo

Renting a Car

I'd like to rent a car.

Quisiera alquilar un coche.

Kee-see-eh-rah ahl-kee-lahr oon coh-cheh

What kind of vehicle?

¿Qué tipo de vehículo?

¿Keh tee-poh deh beh-ee-coo-loh?

We need an economic one.

Necesitamos uno económico.

Neh-seh-see-tah-mohs oo-noh eh-coh-noh-mee-coh.

We need a valid driver's license, official identification and credit card.

Necesitamos licencia de conducir vigente, identificación oficial y tarjeta de crédito.

Neh-seh-see-tah-mohs lee-sehn-see-ah deh cohn-doo-seer vee-gehn-teh, ee-dehn-tee-fee-cah-see-ohn oh-fee-see-ahl ee tahr-jeh-tah deh creh-dee-toh.

What models do you have of this size?

¿Qué modelos tienen de este tamaño?

¿Keh moh-deh-lohs tee-eh-nehn deh ehs-teh tah-mah-nyo?

Do you have an automatic car?

¿Tiene coches automáticos?

¿Tee-eh-neh coh-chehs ah-oo-toh-mah-tee-cohs?

I'd like to rent a manual car.

Quisiera alquilar un coche manual.

Kee-see-eh-rah ahl-kee-lahr oon coh-cheh mah-noo-ahl.

Do you have a car with air conditioning?

¿Tiene un coche con aire acondicionado?

¿Tee-eh-neh oon coh-cheh cohn ah-ee-reh ah-cohn-dee-seeoh-nah-doh?

How much does it cost per day?

¿Cuánto cuesta por día?

¿Kwahn-toh kwehs-tah pohr dee-ah?

Does the price include the insurance?

¿El precio incluye el seguro?

¿El preh-see-oh een-cloo-yeh el seh-goo-roh?

What types of insurance are there?

¿Qué tipos de seguros hay?

¿Keh tee-pohs de seh-goo-rohs i?

How much does the insurance cost?

¿Cuánto cuesta el seguro?

¿Kwahn-toh kwehs-tah el seh-goo-roh?

What incidents does basic insurance cover?

¿Qué incidentes cubre el seguro básico?

¿Keh een-see-dehn-tehs coo-breh el seh-goo-roh bah-see-coh?

How much is the excess?

¿Cuánto es la franquicia?

¿Kwahn-toh ehs lah frahn-kee-see-ah?

Can I travel to other countries?

¿Puedo viajar a otros países?

¿Pwe-doh vee-ah-jahr ah oh-trohs pah-ee-sehs?

Which countries can I travel to?

¿A qué países puedo viajar?

¿A keh pah-ee-sehs pwe-doh vee-ah-jahr?

Where can I return the car?

¿Dónde puedo entregar el coche?

¿Dohn-de pwe-doh ehn-treh-gahr el coh-cheh?

Do I get the car with a full tank?

¿Recibo el coche con el tanque lleno?

¿Reh-see-boh ehl coh-cheh cohn ehl tahn-keh yeh-noh?

Should I return the car with the tank full of gas?

¿Tengo que entregar el coche con el tanque lleno?

¿Tehn-goh que ehn-treh-gahr el coh-cheh cohn ehl tahn-keh yeh-noh?

How much does it cost to include a second driver?

¿Cuánto cuesta incluir un segundo conductor?

¿Kwahn-toh kwehs-tah een-cloo-eer oon seh-goon-doh cohn-dooc-tohr?

Is there a surcharge if I return the car to another office/town/country?

¿Hay un sobreprecio si entrego el coche en otra oficina/ciudad/país?

¿I oon soh-breh-<u>preh</u>-see-oh see ehn-<u>treh</u>-goh ehl <u>coh</u>-cheh ehn <u>oh</u>-trah oh-fee-<u>see</u>-nah/see-oo-<u>dahd</u>/pah-<u>ees</u>?

What type of gas does this car take?

¿Qué tipo de gasolina lleva este auto?

¿Keh <u>tee</u>-poh deh gah-soh-<u>lee</u>-nah <u>yeh</u>-vah <u>ehs</u>-teh <u>ah-oo</u>-toh?

Driving a Car

Where is the next gas station?
¿En dónde se encuentra la siguiente gasolinera?
¿Ehn dohn-deh se ehn-kwehn-trah lah see-guee-ehn-teh gah-soh-lee-neh-rah?

What is the speed limit in cities/on highways?
¿Cuál es la velocidad máxima en la ciudad/en carreteras?
¿Kwahl ehs lah veh-loh-see-dahd mah-xee-mah ehn lah see-oo-dahd/ehn cah-reh-teh-rahs?

Can I park here?
¿Puedo aparcar aquí?
¿Pweh-deh ah-pahr-cahr a-kee?

How long can I park here for?
¿Cuánto tiempo se puede aparcar aquí?
¿Kwahn-toh tee-ehm-poh seh pweh-deh ah-pahr-cahr a-kee?

How much does it cost to park here?
¿Cuánto cuesta el aparcamiento?
¿Kwahn-toh kwehs-tah el ah-pahr-cah-mee-ehn-toh?

I've run out of gas.
Me quedé sin gasolina.
Meh keh-deh seen gah-soh-lee-nah.

Fill it up.
Llene el tanque.
Yeh-neh el tahn-keh.

Check the oil.
Revise el nivel de aceite.
Reh-vee-seh ehl nee-vehl deh ah-seh-ee-teh.

Where can I check my tire pressure?
¿Dónde puedo revisar la presión de las llantas?
¿Dohn-deh pweh-doh reh-vee-sahr lah preh-see-ohn deh lahs yahn-tahs?

Where should I pay?
¿Dónde pago?

¿Dohn-deh pah-goh?

Are the roads paved in this area?

¿Las carreteras están asfaltadas en esta zona?

¿Las cah-reh-teh-rahs ehs-tahn ahs-fahlt-tah-dahs ehn ehs-tah zoh-nah?

Where can I find a mechanic?

¿Dónde puedo encontrar a un mecánico?

¿Dohn-deh pweh-doh ehn-cohn-trahr ah uhn meh-cah-nee-coh?

My car doesn't start.

Mi coche no arranca.

Mi coh-cheh noh ah-rahn-cah

The battery died.

La batería no arranca.

Lah bah-teh-ree-ah noh ah-rahn-cah

I have a flat tire.

Tengo una llanta pinchada.

Tehn-goh oo-nah yahn-tah pin-chah-dah

The car is damaged.

El coche se encuentra dañado.

El coh-cheh se ehn-kwehn-trah dah-nya-doh

Can you fix it?

¿Puede arreglarlo?

¿Pweh-deh ah-reh-glahr-loh?

How much does it cost to fix it?

¿Cuánto cuesta el arreglo?

¿Kwahn-toh kwehs-tah ehl ah-reh-gloh?

Do you have that part?

¿Tiene el repuesto?

¿Tee-eh-neh ehl reh-pwehs-toh?

How long will it take?

¿Cuánto tardará?

¿Kwahn-toh tahr-dah-rah?

Do you have maps of the area?

¿Tiene mapas de la zona?

¿Tee-eh-neh mah-pahs deh lah zoh-nah?

Is this the road to Acapulco?

¿Por aquí se va Acapulco?

¿Por a-kee seh vah ah Acapulco (ah-kah-puhl-koh)?

How do I get to the highway to Santiago?

¿Cómo se llega a la carretera a Santiago?

¿Coh-moh seh yeh-gah ah lah cah-reh-teh-rah ah Santiago (sahn-tee-ah-goh)?

Taking Public Transport

Where is the bus station, please?
¿Dónde está la estación de autobuses, por favor?
¿Dohn-deh ehs-tah lah ehs-tah-see-ohn deh ah-oo-toh-boo-sehs, pohr fah-vohr?

Where is the train station, please?
¿Dónde está la estación de tren, por favor?
¿Dohn-deh ehs-tah lah ehs-tah-see-ohn deh trehn, pohr fah-vohr?

What is the best way to get to the airport, please?
¿Cuál es la mejor manera de llegar al aeropuerto, por favor?
¿Kwahl ehs lah meh-johr mah-neh-rah deh yeh-gahr ahl ah-eh-roh-pwehr-to, pohr fah-vohr?

How far is the beach from here/the hotel, please?
¿A qué distancia está la playa desde aquí/el hotel, por favor?
¿Ah keh dees-tahn-see-ah ehs-tah lah plah-yah dehs-deh ah-kee/ehl oh-tehl, pohr fah-vohr?

How do I get to the beach, please?
¿Por dónde se va a la playa, por favor?
¿Pohr dohn-deh seh vah ah lah plah-yah, pohr fah-vohr?

How do I get to the tourist office, please?
¿Por dónde se va a la oficina de turismo?
¿Pohr dohn-deh seh vah ah lah oh-fee-see-nah deh too-rees-moh?

Is this the train for...?
¿Es este el tren para...?
¿Ehs ehs-teh el trehn pah-rah...?

What time does the train leave for...?
¿A qué hora sale el tren para...?
¿Ah keh oh-rah sah-leh ehl trehn pah-rah...?

What time does the train arrive?
¿A qué hora llega el tren?
¿Ah keh oh-rah yeh-gah ehl trehn?

Where does the bus to Guadalajara leave from?

73

¿De dónde sale el autobús para Guadalajara?
¿Deh dohn-deh sah-leh ehl ah-oo-toh-boos pah-rah Guadalajara (goo-ah-dah-lah-hah-rah)?

Two tickets to Playa del Carmen.
Dos boletos a Playa del Carmen.
Dohs boh-leh-tohs a Playa del Carmen (plah-yah dehl cahr-mehn)

When is the next bus?
¿Cuándo es el próximo autobús?
¿Kwahn-doh ehs ehl proh-xih-moh ah-oo-toh-boos?

When is the last bus?
¿Cuándo es el último autobús?
¿Kwahn-doh ehs ehl ool-tee-moh ah-oo-toh-boos?

Where can I buy a ticket?
¿Dónde se compran los boletos?
¿Dohn-deh seh cohm-prahn los boh-leh-tohs?

Where is the ticket office?
¿Dónde está la taquilla/boletería?
¿Dohn-deh ehs-tah lah tah-kee-yah/boh-leh-teh-ree-ah?

Do I buy the tickets beforehand?
¿Se compran los boletos antes?
¿Seh cohm-prahn los boh-leh-tohs ahn-tehs?

How much is the bus ticket to Lima?
¿Cuánto sale el boleto a Lima?
¿Kwahn-toh sah-leh ehl boh-leh-toh a Lima (lee-mah)?

Don't you have cheaper tickets?
¿No hay boletos más baratos?
¿Noh i boh-leh-tohs mahs bah-rah-tohs?

Is this bus going downtown?
¿Este autobús va al centro?
¿Ehs-teh ah-oo-toh-boos vah ahl cehn-troh?

Can you show me where it is on the map?
¿Me puede mostrar su ubicación en el mapa?
¿Me pwe-deh mohs-trahr soo oo-bee-cah-see-ohn ehn ehl mah-pah?

Does this bus/train stop at…?
¿Éste autobús/tren se detiene en…?
¿Ehs-teh ah-oo-toh-boos/trehn seh deh-tee-eh-neh ehn…?

Is it a direct route?
¿Es un viaje directo?
¿Es un vee-ah-jeh dee-rehc-toh?

Do I have to change buses?
¿Tengo que cambiar de autobús?
¿Tehn-goh keh cahm-bee-ahr deh ah-oo-toh-boos?

How long to get to downtown?
¿Cuánto falta para llegar al centro?
¿Kwahn-toh fahl-tah pah-rah yeh-gahr ahl cehn-troh?

How many stops are there to downtown?
¿Cuántas paradas son al centro?
¿Kwahn-tahs pah-rah-das sohn ahl cehn-troh?

Can you tell me when we get to downtown?
¿Me puede avisar cuando lleguemos al centro?
¿Meh pwe-deh ah-vee-sahr kwahn-doh yeh-gueh-mohs al cehn-troh?

Is this seat taken?
¿Está ocupado este asiento?
¿Ehs-tah oh-coo-pah-doh ehs-teh ah-see-ehn-toh?

My luggage is still on board!
¡Mi equipaje todavía está a bordo!
¡Mee eh-kee-pah-jeh toh-dah-vee-ah ehs-tah ah bohr-doh!

Take my seat.
Toma mi asiento.
Toh-mah mee ah-see-ehn-toh

Does this seat recline?
¿Este asiento se reclina?
¿Ehs-teh ah-see-ehn-toh seh reh-clee-nah?

Would you like to swap seats with me?
¿Quieres intercambiar asientos?
¿Kee-eh-rehs een-tehr-cahm-bee-ahr ah-see-ehn-tohs?

I would like a window seat.

Me gustaría un asiento junto a la ventanilla.
Me goos-tah-ree-ah oon ah-see-ehn-toh hoon-toh ah lah vehn-tah-nee-yah

I want to get off here.
Aquí me bajo.
Ah-kee meh bah-joh

Open the back door.
Abre la puerta de atrás.
Ah-breh lah pwer-tah deh ah-trahs

Do you have a timetable?
¿Tienes un cronograma?
¿Tee-eh-nehs oon croh-noh-grah-mah?

How often do trains come?
¿Cada cuánto viene el tren?
¿Cah-dah kwahn-toh vee-eh-neh ehl trehn?

Has the train been cancelled?
¿Cancelaron el tren?
¿Cahn-seh-lah-rohn ehl trehn?

I've lost my ticket.
Perdí mi boleto.
Pehr-dee mee boh-leh-toh

What time does it start?
¿A qué hora empieza?
¿Ah keh oh-rah ehm-pee-eh-sah?

Is there a subway here?
¿Hay un metro aquí?
¿Hay oon meh-troh ah-kee?

Where is the closest underground station?
¿Dónde está la estación más cercana?
¿Dohn-deh ehs-tah lah ehs-tah-see-on mass cehr-cah-nah?

How much is the fare/token?
¿Cuánto es la tarifa?
¿Kwahn-toh ehs lah tah-ree-fah?

Do I need exact change?
¿Necesito tener cambio exacto?

¿Neh-seh-<u>see</u>-toh teh-<u>nehr</u> <u>cahm</u>-bee-oh eh-<u>xahc</u>-toh?

Which is the line that goes to the mall?

¿Cuál es la línea que va al centro comercial?

¿Kwahl ehs lah <u>lee</u>-neh-ah keh vah ahl <u>cehn</u>-troh coh-mehr-<u>see-ahl</u>?

Taking a Taxi

Do you know the number to call a taxi?
¿Conoce el número de algún servicio de taxis?
¿Coh-noh-seh ehl noo-meh-roh deh ahl-goon sehr-vee-see-oh deh taxis?

I would like a taxi at 10 am.
Quisiera un taxi a las 10 de la mañana.
Kee-see-eh-rah un taxi ah lahs 10 deh lah mah-nya-nah

I need a taxi as soon as possible.
Necesito un taxi tan pronto como sea posible.
Neh-seh-see-toh un taxi tahn prohn-toh coh-moh seh-ah poh-see-bleh

Is this taxi free?
¿Está libre el taxi?
¿Ehs-tah lee-breh el taxi?

I need to go to the National Museum.
Necesito ir al Museo Nacional.
Neh-seh-see-toh eer ahl moo-seh-oh nah-see-oh-nahl

How much to go to the beach?
¿Cuál es el precio para ir a la playa?
¿Kwahl ehs ehl preh-see-oh pah-rah eer ah lah plah-yah?

Do you have a meter?
¿Tiene un taxímetro?
¿Tee-eh-neh oon tahk-see-meh-troh?

Can you stop here?
¿Puede detenerse aquí?
¿Pwe-deh deh-teh-nehr-seh ah-kee?

Wait here.
Espere aquí.
Ehs-peh-reh ah-kee

Stop at the next traffic light.
Déjeme en el próximo semáforo.
Deh-jeh-meh ehn ehl proh-xeeh-moh seh-mah-foh-roh

Go straight ahead.

Siga derecho.
See-gah deh-reh-choh

Turn at the corner.
Gire en la esquina.
Jee-reh ehn lah ehs-kee-nah

Turn to the left.
Gire a la izquierda.
Jee-reh ah lah ees-kee-ehr-dah

Turn to the right.
Gire a la derecha.
Jee-reh ah lah de-reh-chah

Go to the next crossroad.
Vaya al primer cruce.
Vah-yah ahl pree-mehr croo-ceh

Getting Around: Asking for Directions

Is there a pharmacy nearby?
¿Hay una farmacia cerca?
¿I oo-nah fahr-mah-see-ah sehr-cah?

Is it far from here?
¿Está lejos?
¿Ehs-tah leh-johs?

How do I get to downtown?
¿Cómo llego al centro?
¿Coh-moh yeh-goh ahl sehn-troh?

I'm looking for this street.
Busco esta calle.
Boos-coh ehs-tah cah-yeh

How far is it?
¿A cuánto está?
¿Ah kwahn-toh ehs-tah?

It's straight ahead.
Siga derecho.
See-gah deh-reh-choh

Turn right at the next corner.
Dobla a la derecha en la próxima esquina.
Doh-blah ah lah deh-reh-chah ehn lah proh-xeeh-mah ehs-kee-nah

Turn left at the traffic lights.
Dobla a la izquierda en el semáforo.
Doh-blah ah lah ees-kee-ehr-da ehn ehl seh-mah-foh-roh

The supermarket is in front of the park.
El supermercado está frente al parque.
Ehl soo-pehr-mehr-cah-doh ehs-tah frehn-teh ahl pahr-keh

The restaurant is next to the church.
El restaurante está a lado de la iglesia.

Ehl rehs-tah-oo-rahn-teh ehs-tah ah lah-doh deh lah ee-gleh-see-ah

It's close.

Está cerca.

Ehs-tah sehr-cah

It's far.

Está lejos.

Ehs-tah leh-johs

How can I get there?

¿Cómo se llega hasta allá?

¿Coh-mo seh yeh-gah ahs-tah ah-yah?

Is there still time to get there?

¿Todavía hay tiempo para llegar?

¿Toh-dah-vee-ah I tee-ehm-poh pah-rah yeh-gahr?

I'm in a hurry.

Tengo prisa.

Tehn-goh pree-sah

There's plenty of time.

Hay tiempo de sobra.

I tee-ehm-poh deh soh-brah

Is it possible to walk there?

¿Es posible caminar hasta allá?

¿Ehs poh-see-bleh cah-mee-nahr ahs-tah ah-yah?

Is this area safe past midnight?

¿Es segura la zona después de medianoche?

¿Ehs seh-goo-rah lah zoh-nah dehs-pwehs deh meh-dee-ah-noh-cheh?

At the Hotel

Can you recommend a cheap hotel?

¿Me puede recomendar un hotel barato?

¿Me pwe-deh reh-coh-mehn-dahr oon oh-tehl bah-rah-toh?

Is there a youth hostel in the area?

¿Hay un albergue juvenil en el área?

¿I oon ahl-behr-gueh hoo-veh-neel ehn ehl ah-reh-ah?

I have booked a room.

He reservado una habitación.

Eh reh-sehr-vah-doh oo-nah ah-bee-tah-see-ohn

I made the reservation through Booking.

Reservé a través de Booking.

Reh-sehr-veh ah trah-vehs deh Booking

Can you give me the key to my room?

¿Puedes darme la llave de mi habitación?

¿Pwe-dehs darh-meh lah yah-veh deh mee ah-bee-tah-see-ohn?

This room is too noisy.

Esta habitación es demasiado ruidosa.

Ehs-tah ah-bee-tah-see-ohn ehs deh-mah-see-ah-doh roo-ee-doh-sah

Do you have a firmer mattress?

¿No tiene un colchón más duro?

¿No tee-eh-neh oon cohl-chohn mahs doo-roh?

I'd like a room with a nice view.

Me gustaría una habitación con una linda vista.

Meh goos-tah-ree-ah oo-nah ah-bee-tah-see-ohn con oo-nah leen-dah vees-tah

I'd like to order room service.

Quisiera pedir servicio a la habitación.

Kee-see-eh-rah peh-dihr sehr-bee-see-oh a la ah-bee-tah-see-ohn

When is check-out time?

¿Cuándo es la hora límite de salida?

¿Kwahn-doh ehs lah oh-rah lee-mee-teh deh sah-lee-dah?

How was your stay with us?

¿Qué les ha parecido su estancia con nosotros?

¿Keh lehs ah pah-reh-see-doh soo ehs-tahn-see-ah cohn noh-soh-trohs?

Very nice, thanks.

Muy agradable, gracias.

Mooy ah-grah-dah-ble, grah-see-ahs

Here is your bill, please look it over.

Aquí tiene su factura. Por favor revísela.

Ah-kee tee-eh-neh soo fahc-too-rah. Pohr fah-vohr reh-vee-seh-lah

Is there a swimming pool?

¿Hay una piscina?

¿I oo-nah pee-see-nah?

Do you have any rooms available?

¿Le queda alguna habitación?

¿Leh keh-dah al-goo-nah ah-bee-tah-see-ohn?

Does the hotel have Internet access?

¿Tiene el hotel acceso a Internet?

¿Tee-eh-neh el oh-tehl ahx-seh-soh ah internet?

I'd like a room.

Quiero una habitación.

Kee-eh-roh oo-nah ah-bee-tah-see-ohn

I would like a room with a shower.

Quiero una habitación con ducha.

Kee-eh-roh oo-nah ah-bee-tah-see-ohn cohn doo-chah

Does it have a private bathroom?

¿Tiene baño privado?

¿Tee-eh-neh bah-nyo pree-vah-doh?

How much is a single/double room per night?

¿Cúanto cuesta un habitación individual/doble por noche?

¿Kwahn-toh kwehs-tah oo-nah ah-bee-tah-see-ohn een-dee-vee-doo-ahl/doh-bleh pohr noh-cheh?

I'm locked out of my room.

Quedé encerrado fuera de la habitación.
Keh-deh ehn-seh-rah-doh fweh-ra deh lah ah-bee-tah-see-ohn.

Our door is jammed.

La puerta se atascó.
Lah pwehr-tah seh ah-tahs-coh

Can you show me to my room?

¿Me podrías acompañar a mi habitación?
¿Me poh-dree-ahs ah-cohm-pah-nyar a mee ah-bee-tah-see-ohn?

I would like a double room.

Quiero una habitación doble.
Kee-eh-roh oo-nah ah-bee-tah-see-ohn doh-bleh

Is breakfast included?

¿Incluye el desayuno?
¿Een-cloo-yeh ehl deh-sah-yoo-noh?

At what time is breakfast served?

¿A qué hora se sirve el desayuno?
¿Ah keh oh-rah seh seer-veh ehl deh-sah-yoo-noh?

Is there a restaurant in the hotel?

¿Hay restaurante en el hotel?
¿I rehs-tah-oo-rahn-teh ehn ehl oh-tehl?

Is there a lift/elevator?

¿Hay ascensor en el hotel?
¿I ah-sehn-sohr ehn ehl oh-tehl?

Is there another hotel near here?

¿Hay otro hotel cerca de aquí?
¿I oh-troh oh-tehl sehr-cah deh ah-kee?

What time does the hotel close in the evenings?

¿A qué hora cierran la puerta de entrada?
¿Ah keh oh-rah see-eh-rahn lah pwehr-tah deh ehn-trah-dah?

When is dinner served?

¿A qué hora es la cena?
¿Ah keh oh-rah ehs lah ceh-nah?

Could you please wake me up at 7:00 o'clock?
¿Me podría despertar a las siete de la mañana, por favor?
¿Meh poh-<u>dree-ah</u> dehs-pehr-<u>tahr</u> ah lahs <u>see-eh</u>-teh deh lah mah-<u>nya</u>-nah, porh fah-<u>vohr</u>?

Could you send me a towel to my room, please?
¿Me podría enviar una toalla, por favor?
¿Meh poh-<u>dree-ah</u> ehn-<u>bee-ahr</u> <u>oo</u>-nah toh-<u>ah</u>-yah porh fah-<u>vohr</u>?

There is no toilet paper in my room.
No hay papel higiénico en mi habitación.
Noh I pah-<u>pehl</u> ee-<u>he-eh</u>-nee-coh ehn mee ah-bee-tah-<u>see-ohn</u>

The TV is not working.
El televisor no está funcionando.
Ehl teh-leh-vee-<u>sohr</u> noh ehs-<u>tah</u> foon-see-oh-<u>nahn</u>-doh

The room is very dark.
La habitación es muy oscura.
Lah ah-bee-tah-<u>see-ohn</u> ehs mooy ohs-<u>coo</u>-rah

It's very noisy.
Hay mucho ruido.
I <u>moo</u>-choh <u>roo-ee</u>-doh

The air conditioner isn't working.
El aire acondicionado no funciona.
Ehl <u>ah-ee</u>-reh ah-cohn-dee-see-oh-<u>nah</u>-doh noh foon-<u>see</u>-oh-nah

The faucet is dripping.
El grifo gotea.
Eh <u>gree</u>-foh goh-<u>teh</u>-ah

Could you send someone to collect my bags?
¿Podría mandar a alguien para bajar mi equipaje?
¿Poh-<u>dree-ah</u> mah-<u>dahr</u> ah <u>ahl</u>-guee-ehn <u>pah</u>-rah bah-<u>hahr</u> mee eh-kee-<u>pah</u>-heh?

Could you give me my key, please?
¿Me podría dar mi llave, por favor?
¿Meh poh-<u>dree-ah</u> dahr mee <u>yah</u>-veh, porh fah-<u>vohr</u>?

Are there movies in English on the TV?

¿Hay películas en inglés en la tele?

¿I peh-lee-coo-lahs ehn een-glehs ehn lah teh-leh?

Is this free?

¿Es gratis esto?

¿Ehs grah-tees ehs-toh?

Do you charge for local calls placed from the room?

¿Cobran llamadas locales desde el cuarto?

¿Coh-brahn yah-mah-dahs loh-cah-lehs dehs-deh ehl kwahr-toh?

Is there wifi in my room?

¿Hay wifi en mi cuarto?

¿I wifi ehn mee kwahr-toh?

What is the password?

¿Cuál es la contraseña?

¿Kwahl ehs lah cohn-trah-seh-nya?

Are pets allowed at the hotel?

¿Admiten mascotas en el hotel?

¿Ahd-mee-tehn mahs-coh-tahs ehn ehl oh-tehl?

How much is the deposit?

¿Cuál es el depósito?

¿Kwahl ehs ehl deh-poh-see-toh?

Is the tap water drinkable?

¿Puedo tomar el agua del grifo?

¿Pwe-doh toh-mahr ehl ah-wah dehl gree-foh?

Do you have a bigger room?

¿Tienen una habitación más grande?

¿Tee-eh-nehn oo-nah ah-bee-tah-see-ohn mahs grahn-deh?

I need to speak to your manager.

Necesito hablar con el supervisor.

Neh-seh-see-toh ah-blahr cohn ehl soo-pehr-vee-sohr.

Do you have a charger for this laptop?

¿Tienen un cargador para esta laptop?

¿Tee-eh-nehn oon cahr-gah-dohr pah-rah ehs-tah laptop?

Where can I get a compatible adapter?

¿Dónde puedo conseguir un adaptador compatible?

¿Dohn-deh pwe-doh cohn-seh-gueer oon ah-dahp-tah-dohr cohm-pah-tee-bleh?

Do you have a mini-USB cord?
¿Tienen un cable mini USB?

¿Tee-eh-nehn oon cah-bleh mini oo-ese-beh?

Where can I plug this in?
¿Dónde puedo conectar esto?

¿Dohn-deh pwe-doh coh-nehc-tahr ehs-toh?

I need to borrow an HDMI cord.
Necesito un cable HDMI.

Neh-seh-see-toh oon cah-bleh ah-cheh-deh-eh-meh-ee.

Could I check out later?
¿Podría dejar la habitación más tarde?

¿Poh-dree-ah deh-hahr la ah-bee-tah-see-ohn mahs tahr-deh?

Can I leave my luggage until 6?
¿Puedo dejar mi equipaje hasta las 6?

¿Pwe-doh deh-hahr mee eh-kee-pah-heh ahs-tah lahs seh-ees?

Could you call me a taxi to the airport?
¿Podría pedirme un taxi al aeropuerto?

¿Poh-dree-ah peh-deer-meh oon taxi ahl ah-eh-roh-poo-ehr-toh?

At the Airport

Your passports, please.
Sus pasaportes, por favor.
Soos pah-sah-pohr-tehs, pohr fah-vohr

We are traveling together.
Estamos viajando juntos.
Ehs-tah-mohs vee-ah-hahn-doh hoon-tohs

When is the next flight to...?
¿Cuándo sale el próximo vuelo para...?
¿Kwahn-doh sah-leh ehl proh-xee-moh bweh-loh pah-rah...?

Where is the boarding gate?
¿Dónde está la puerta de embarque?
¿Dohn-deh ehs-tah lah pwehr-tah de ehm-bar-keh?

Has the flight been canceled?
¿Se ha cancelado el vuelo?
¿Se ha cahn-seh-lah-doh el bweh-loh?

I need a ticket to...
Necesito un billete para...
Neh-seh-see-toh un bee-yeh-teh pah-rah...

Is this the check-in for flight...?
¿Es este el mostrador de check-in del vuelo...?
¿Ehs ehs-teh ehl mohs-trah-dohr deh check-in dehl bweh-loh...?

I would like to change my reservation.
Querría cambiar mi reserva.
Keh-ree-ah cahm-bee-ahr mee reh-sehr-vah

I would like to confirm my reservation.
Querría confirmar mi reserva.
Keh-ree-ah cohn-feer-mahr mee reh-sehr-vah

I would like to cancel my reservation.
Querría anular mi reserva.
Keh-ree-ah ah-noo-lahr mee reh-sehr-vah

Where is the airport?

¿Dónde está el aeropuerto?

¿Dohn-deh ehs-tah ehl ah-eh-roh-pwehr-toh?

Where is the international terminal?

¿Dónde está la terminal internacional?

¿Dohn-deh ehs-tah lah tehr-mee-nahl een-tehr-nah-see-oh-nahl?

I'm looking for terminal 1.

Busco la terminal 1.

Boos-coh lah tehr-mee-nahl 1 (oo-no)

This terminal is for international flights.

Esta terminal es para vuelos internacionales.

Ehs-tah tehr-mee-nahl es pah-rah bweh-lohs een-tehr-nah-see-oh-nah-les

Is this the terminal for local flights?

¿Es esta la terminal para vuelos nacionales?

¿Ehs ehs-tah lah tehr-mee-nahl pah-rah bweh-lohs nah-see-oh-nah-les?

Where can I find the luggage carts?

¿Dónde están los carritos de equipaje?

¿Dohn-deh ehs-tahn lohs cah-ree-tohs deh eh-kee-pah-heh?

We need help to get on the plane.

Necesitamos ayuda para subir al avión.

Neh-seh-see-tah-mohs a-yoo-dah pah-rah soo-beer ahl ah-vee-ohn

This is my carry-on baggage.

Este es mi equipaje de mano.

Ehs-teh ehs mee eh-kee-pah-heh deh mah-noh

Can I take this as carry-on luggage?

¿Puedo llevar esto como equipaje de mano?

¿Pwe-doh yeh-vahr ehs-toh coh-moh eh-kee-pah-heh deh mah-noh?

I have two bags with me.

Llevo dos malestas.

Yeh-voh dohs mah-leh-tahs

Where can I claim my luggage?

¿Dónde puedo reclamar mi equipaje?
¿Dohn-deh pwe-doh reh-clah-mahr mee eh-kee-pah-heh?

My luggage hasn't arrived.
Mis maletas no llegaron.
Mees mah-leh-tahs noh yeh-gah-rohn

My luggage is lost.
Se perdió mi equipaje.
Seh pehr-dee-oh mee eh-kee-pah-heh

I want to change my seat.
Quisiera cambiar mi asiento.
Kee-see-eh-rah cahm-bee-ahr mi ah-see-ehn-toh

The plane's arrival is delayed.
El avión llega con retraso.
El ah-vee-ohn yeh-gah cohn reh-trah-soh

The plane's departure is delayed.
El avión sale con retraso.
El ah-vee-ohn sah-leh cohn reh-trah-soh

It's a flight with an intermediate stop in...
Es un vuelo con escala en...
Ehs oon bweh-loh cohn ehs-cah-lah ehn...

It's a nonstop flight.
Es un vuelo directo / Es un vuelo sin escalas.
*Ehs oon bweh-loh dee-rec-toh / Ehs oon bweh-loh seen
ehs-cah-lahs*

Last call for passengers of flight 1234 to destination...
Última llamada a los pasajeros del vuelo 1234 con destino...
*Ool-tee-mah yah-mah-dah ah lohs pah-sah-heh-rohs dehl
bweh-loh 1234 (oo-no dohs trehs kwah-troh) cohn dehs-
tee-noh...*

Where is customs?
¿Dónde está la aduana?
¿Dohn-deh ehs-tah lah ah-dwah-nah?

Do you have anything to declare?
¿Tiene algo que declarar?
¿Tee-eh-neh ahl-goh keh deh-clah-rahr?

I have nothing to declare.
No tengo nada que declarar.
No tehn-goh nah-dah keh deh-clah-rahr

How long do you intend to stay here?
¿Cuánto tiempo piensa estar aquí?
¿Kwahn-toh tee-ehm-poh pee-ehn-sah ehs-tahr ah-kee?

I'll be staying here a few days.
Estaré aquí unos días
Ehs-tah-reh ah-kee oo-nohs dee-ahs

I'm here in transit (only passing through).
Estoy aquí de tránsito.
Ehs-toy ah-kee deh trahn-see-toh

What is the purpose of your visit?
¿Cuál es el propósito de su visita?
¿Kwahl ehs ehl proh-poh-see-toh deh soo vee-see-tah?

I'm here on vacation.
Estoy aquí de vacaciones.
Ehs-toy ah-kee deh vah-cah-see-ohn-ehs

I'm here on business.
Estoy aquí en viaje de negocios.
Ehs-toy ah-kee en vee-ah-heh deh neh-goh-see-ohs

Is there a bus to the city center?
¿Hay un autobús al centro?
¿I oon ah-oo-toh-boos ahl cehn-troh?

I need a taxi to the ... Hotel.
Necesito un taxi al Hotel ...
Neh-seh-see-toh oon taxi ahl oh-tehl...

Could you tell me if this is the flight to...?
¿Podría decirme si este es el vuelo a...?
¿Poh-dree-ah deh-seer-meh see ehs-teh ehs ehl bweh-loh ah...?

When is the next plane to...?
¿Cuándo sale el próximo avión a...?
¿Kwahn-doh sah-leh ehl proh-xee-moh ah-vee-ohn ah...?

Do you have first-class tickets available?

¿Tiene boletos de primera clase?

¿Tee-eh-neh boh-leh-tohs deh pree-meh-rah clah-seh?

I'm an American citizen.

Soy ciudadano americano.

Soy see-oo-dah-dah-noh ah-meh-ree-cah-noh

We're tourists on vacation.

Somos turistas de vacaciones.

Soh-mohs too-rees-tahs deh vah-cah-see-oh-nehs

I'm looking for an apartment.

Busco un apartamento.

Boos-coh oon ah-pahr-tah-mehn-toh

This is a short-term stay.

Nos quedaremos poco tiempo.

Nos keh-dah-reh-mohs poh-coh tee-ehm-poh

I'm looking for a place to rent.

Necesito un lugar para alquilar.

Neh-seh-see-toh oon loo-gahr pah-rah ahl-kee-lahr

We need the cheapest place you have.

Necesitamos el lugar más económico que tenga.

Neh-seh-see-tah-mohs ehl loo-gahr mahs eh-coh-noh-mee-coh keh tehn-gah

Celebrating

Happy birthday!
¡Feliz cumpleaños!
¡Feh-lees coom-pleh-ah-nyos!

Merry Christmas!
¡Feliz Navidad!
¡Feh-lees nah-vee-dahd!

Happy new year!
¡Feliz año nuevo!
¡Feh-lees ah-nyo noo-eh-voh!

See you next year!
¡Nos vemos el próximo año!
¡Nohs veh-mohs ehl proh-xee-moh ah-nyo!

Happy holidays!
¡Felices vacaciones!
¡Feh-lee-sehs vah-cah-see-oh-nehs!

Best wishes for the new year!
¡Mis mejores deseos para el año nuevo!
¡Mees meh-hoh-rehs de-seh-ohs pah-rah ehl ah-nyo noo-eh-voh!

Happy Easter!
¡Felices Pascuas!
¡Feh-lee-sehs pahs-kwahs!

Happy Valentine's day!
¡Feliz día de San Valentín!
¡Feh-lees dee-ah deh sahn vah-lehn-teen!

Happy Mother's day!
¡Feliz día de la Madre!
¡Feh-lees dee-ah deh lah mah-dreh!

Happy Father's day!
¡Feliz día del Padre!
¡Feh-lees dee-ah dehl pah-dreh!

Congratulations!
¡Felicidades! ¡Enhorabuena!

¡Feh-lee-see-<u>dah</u>-dehs! ¡Ehn-oh-rah-<u>boo-eh</u>-nah!

Welcome!
¡Bienvenido/a!

¡Bee-ehn-veh-<u>nee</u>-doh/ah!

Have a nice trip!
¡Buen viaje!

¡Bwehn <u>vee-ah</u>-jeh!

School

Where do you study?
¿Dónde estudias?
¿Dohn-deh ehs-too-dee-ahs?

What days do you go to school/college?
¿Qué días vas a la escuela/universidad?
¿Keh dee-ahs vahs ah lah ehs-kweh-lah/oo-nee-vehr-see-dahd?

I go from Monday to Friday.
Voy de lunes a viernes.
Vohy deh loo-nehs ah vee-ehr-nehs

What time do you start classes?
¿A qué hora comienzas las clases?
¿Ah keh oh-rah coh-mee-ehn-sahs lahs clah-sehs?

I start at 8 in the morning.
Comienzo a las 8 de la mañana.
Coh-mee-ehn-soh ah lahs oh-cho deh lah mah-nya-nah

How many classes are you taking this semester?
¿Cuántas clases llevas este semestre?
¿Kwahn-tahs clah-sehs yeh-vahs ehs-teh seh-mehs-treh?

I'm taking eight classes.
Llevo ocho clases.
Yeh-voh oh-choh clah-sehs

What classes are you taking this year?
¿Qué clases estás llevando/tomando este año?
¿Keh clah-sehs ehs-tahs yeh-vahn-doh/toh-mahn-doh ehs-teh ah-nyo?

What is your favorite class?
¿Cuál es tu clase favorita?
¿Kwahl es tu clah-seh fah-voh-ree-tah?

What is the most difficult class for you?
¿Cuál es la clase más difícil para ti?
¿Kwahl es la clah-seh mahs dee-fee-ceel pah-rah tee?

What is the name of your Spanish teacher?

¿Cómo se llama tu profesor de español?

¿Coh-moh seh yah-mah too proh-feh-sohr deh ehs-pah-nyol?

His name is Juan.

Se llama Juan.

Seh yah-mah Juan

When is the essay due?

¿Cuándo debo entregar el ensayo?

¿Kwahn-doh deh-boh ehn-treh-gahr ehl ehn-sah-yoh?

I have a test next Wednesday.

Tengo examen el miércoles que viene.

Tehn-goh ehx-sah-mehn ehl mee-er-coh-lehs keh vee-eh-neh

I failed the exam.

Desaprobé el examen.

Dehs-ah-proh-beh ehl ehx-sah-mehn

I passed the test!

¡Aprobé el examen!

¡Ah-proh-beh ehl ehx-sah-mehn!

Where can I get the book?

¿Dónde puedo conseguir el libro?

¿Dohn-deh pwe-doh cohn-seh-geer ehl lee-broh?

How can I get to the library?

¿Cómo llego a la biblioteca?

¿Coh-moh yeh-goh ah lah bee-blee-oh-teh-cah?

I need to borrow this book.

Necesito tomar prestado este libro.

Neh-seh-see-to toh-mahr prehs-tah-doh ehs-teh lee-broh

We went to the campus party.

Fuimos a una fiesta en el campus.

Fwee-mohs ah oo-nah fee-ehs-tah ehn ehl campus

What program are you enrolled in?

¿En qué programa te inscribiste?

¿En keh proh-grah-mah teh eens-cree-bees-teh?

Do you need help studying?

¿Necesitas ayuda para estudiar?

¿Neh-seh-see-tas ah-yoo-dah pah-rah ehs-too-dee-ahr?

Do I have to use pencil or ink?

¿Uso lápiz o bolígrafo?

¿Oo-soh lah-pees oh boh-lee-grah-froh?

Food and Drinks

At a Restaurant

I'd like to see the menu, please.
Quisiera ver el menú, por favor.
Kee-see-eh-rah vehr ehl meh-noo, porh fah-vohr

Could I have...?
¿Me trae...?
¿Meh trah-eh...?

What is on today's menu?
¿Cuál es el menú de hoy?
¿Kwahl ehs ehl meh-noo deh oy?

What do you recommend?
¿Qué me recomienda?
¿Keh meh reh-coh-mee-ehn-da?

What is the house specialty?
¿Cuál es la especialidad de la casa?
¿Kwahl ehs lah ehs-peh-see-ah-lee-dahd deh lah cah-sah?

What is the typical food of this region?
¿Cuál es la comida típica de esta región?
¿Kwahl ehs lah coh-mee-dah tee-pee-cah deh ehs-tah reh-he-on?

Do you have a wine list?
¿Tienen lista de vinos?
¿Tee-eh-nehn lees-tah de vee-nohs?

We need more time to decide.
Necesitamos más tiempo para decidir.
Neh-seh-see-tah-mohs mahs tee-ehm-poh pah-rah deh-see-deer

We would like to have breakfast/lunch/dinner.
Querríamos desayunar/almorzar/cenar.
Keh-ree-ah-mohs deh-sah-yoo-nahr/ahl-mohr-sahr/seh-nahr

I/We are ready to order

Estoy/Estamos listos para ordenar/pedir.

Ehs-toy/Ehs-tah-mohs lees-tohs pah-rah ohr-deh-nahr/peh-deer

I'm allergic to...

Soy alérgico/a a...

Soy ah-lehr-he-coh/ah ah...

I'm vegetarian.

Soy vegetariano/a.

Soy veh-heh-tah-ree-ah-noh/ah

Is this kosher?

¿Es kosher?

¿Ehs kosher?

Does this contain refined sugar?

¿Contiene azúcar refinado?

¿Cohn-tee-eh-neh ah-soo-cahr reh-fee-nah-do?

Do you have options for gluten intolerant people?

¿Tiene opciones para personas intolerantes al gluten?

¿Tee-eh-neh ohp-see-oh-nehs pah-rah pehr-soh-nahs een-toh-leh-rahn-tehs ahl gloo-tehn?

Is this organic food?

¿Es comida orgánica?

¿Ehs coh-mee-dah ohr-gah-nee-cah?

I would like to make a reservation for four people.

Quisiera hacer una reserva para cuatro personas.

Kee-see-eh-rah ah-sehr oo-nah reh-sehr-vha pah-rah kwah-troh pehr-soh-nahs

That was delicious!

¡Estuvo delicioso!

¡Ehs-too-voh deh-lee-see-oh-soh!

This is not what I ordered.

Esto no es lo que he pedido.

Ehs-toh noh ehs loh keh eh peh-dee-doh

No, thank you, I'm full.

No, gracias, estoy lleno/a.

Noh, grah-see-ahs, ehs-toy yeh-noh/ah

Do you have a take-away box?
¿Tienen una caja para llevar?
¿Tee-eh-nehn oo-nah cah-hah pah-rah yeh-vahr?

Is the tip included?
¿La propina está incluida?
¿Lah proh-pee-nah ehs-tah een-cloo-ee-dah?

We'd like to pay together.
Nos gustaría pagar juntos.
Nohs goos-tah-ree-ah pah-gahr hoon-tohs

We'd like to pay separately.
Nos gustaría pagar por separado.
Nohs goos-tah-ree-ah pah-gahr pohr seh-pah-rah-doh

Cash.
Dinero efectivo.
Dee-neh-roh eh-fehc-tee-voh

Do you accept traveler's checks?
¿Acepta cheques de viajero?
¿Ah-cehp-tah che-kehs deh vee-ah-heh-roh?

Do you accept credit cards?
¿Acepta tarjeta de crédito?
¿Ah-cehp-tah tahr-heh-tah deh creh-dee-toh?

Check, please.
La cuenta, por favor.
Lah kwehn-tah, pohr fah-vohr.

Do you serve alcohol?
¿Sirven bebidas con alcohol?
¿Seer-vehn beh-bee-dahs cohn ahl-cohl?

Can we put two tables together?
¿Podríamos juntar dos mesas?
¿Poh-dree-ah-mohs hoon-tahr dohs meh-sahs?

Could you move us to a differnet table?
¿Podríamos cambiar de mesa?
¿Poh-dree-ah-mohs cahm-bee-ahr deh meh-sah?

Do you serve coffee?
¿Sirven café?

¿Seer-vehn cah-feh?

Do you serve soy milk?
¿Tienen leche de soja?
¿Tee-eh-nehn leh-cheh deh soh-hah?

Do you have almond milk?
¿Tienen leche de almendras?
¿Tee-eh-nehn leh-cheh deh ahl-mehn-drahs?

Do you have a kids' menu?
¿Tienen menú infantil?
¿Tee-eh-nehn meh-noo een-fahn-teel?

Could you heat this up?
¿Podría calentar esto?
¿Poh-dree-ah cah-lehn-tahr ehs-toh?

Do you have beer on tap?
¿Sirven cerveza tirada?
¿Seer-vehn sehr-veh-sah tee-rah-dah?

This order is incorrect/I didn't ask for this.
No pedí esto.
Noh peh-dee ehs-toh

This bill is incorrect.
Esta cuenta está mal.
Ehs-tah kwehn-tah ehs-tah mahl

Can you recommend a vegetarian restaurant?
¿Me puede recomendar un restaurante vegetariano?
¿Meh pweh-deh reh-coh-mehn-dahr oon rehs-tah-oo-rahn-teh veh-heh-tah-ree-ah-noh?

Where is the nearest pastry shop?
¿Dónde está la panadería más cercana?
¿Dohn-deh ehs-tah lah pah-nah-deh-ree-ah mahs sehr-cah-nah?

Where can we go for cheap food?
¿Dónde se puede comer barato?
¿Dohn-deh seh poo-eh-deh coh-mehr bah-rah-toh?

What kind of food is sold at this stand?
¿Qué tipo de comida se vende en este puesto?

¿Keh tee-poh deh coh-mee-dah seh vehn-deh ehn ehs-teh pwehs-toh?

Is this sauce spicy?

¿Es picante esta salsa?

¿Ehs pee-cahn-teh ehs-tah sahl-sah?

Common Vocabulary

Wine	Vino	*Vee-noh*
Soda	Gaseosa	*Gah-seh-oh-sah*
Water	Agua	*Ah-wa*
Sparkling water	Agua con gas	*Ah-wa cohn gahs*
Alcohol	Alcohol	*Ahl-cohl*
Apple	Manzana	*Mahn-sah-nah*
Avocado	Aguacate	*Ah-wa-cah-teh*
Bacon	Tocino	*Toh-see-noh*
Banana	Plátano	*Plah-tah-noh*
Barbecue	Barbacoa	*Bahr-bah-coh-ah*
Beef	Carne de vaca	*Cahr-neh deh vah-cah*
Beer	Cerveza	*Cehr-veh-zah*
Bottle	Botella	*Boh-teh-yah*
Bread	Pan	*Pahn*
Butter	Mantequilla	*Mahn-teh-kee-yah*
Cake	Pastel	*Pahs-tehl*
Casserole	Estofado	*Ehs-toh-fah-doh*
Cheese	Queso	*Keh-soh*
Chicken	Pollo	*Poh-yoh*
Chocolate	Chocolate	*Choh-coh-lah-teh*
Cider	Sidra	*See-drah*
Coffee	Café	*Cah-feh*
Cookie	Galleta	*Gah-yeh-tah*
Cream	Crema	*Creh-mah*
Cucumber	Pepino	*Peh-pee-noh*
Cupcake	Magdalena	*Mahg-dah-leh-nah*
Dessert	Postre	*Pohs-treh*

Egg	Huevo	*Oo-eh-voh*
Fish	Pescado	*Pehs-cah-doh*
French fries	Patatas fritas	*Pah-tah-tahs free-tahs*
Garlic	Ajo	*Ah-hoh*
Grill	Asar (a la parrilla)	*Ah-sahr (ah lah pah-ree-yah)*
Ham	Jamón	*Ha-mohn*
Honey	Miel	*Mee-ehl*
Hot dog	Perrito caliente	*Peh-ree-toh cah-lee-ehn-teh*
Ice	Hielo	*Ee-eh-loh*
Ice cream	Helado	*Eh-lah-doh*
Jam	Mermelada	*Mehr-meh-lah-dah*
Juice	Jugo	*Hooh-goh*
Lemon	Limón	*Lee-mohn*
Lentils	Lentejas	*Lehn-teh-has*
Lettuce	Lechuga	*Leh-choo-gah*
Mayonnaise	Mayonesa	*Mah-yoh-neh-sah*
Meat	Carne	*Cahr-neh*
Meatball	Albóndiga	*Ahl-bohn-dee-gah*
Milk	Leche	*Leh-cheh*
Milkshake	Batido (de leche)	*Bah-tee-doh (deh leh-cheh)*
Mushroom	Seta	*Seh-tah*
Mustard	Mostaza	*Mohs-tah-sah*
Olive oil	Aceite de oliva	*Ah-say-teh deh oh-lee-vah*
Onion	Cebolla	*Seh-boh-yah*
Orange	Naranja	*Nah-rahn-hah*
Oregano	Orégano	*Oh-reh-gah-noh*
Pancake	Crepe	*Crehp*
Paprika	Pimentón	*Pee-mehn-tohn*

Parsley	Perejil	*Peh-reh-hill*
Partridge	Perdiz	*Perh-dees*
Pasta	Pasta	*Pahs-tah*
Pasty	Empanada	*Ehm-pah-nah-dah*
Pea	Guisante	*Ghee-sahn-teh*
Peach	Durazno	*Doo-rahs-noh*
Pear	Pera	*Peh-rah*
Pepper	Pimienta	*Pee-mee-ehn-tah*
Pineapple	Piña	*Pee-nya*
Plum	Ciruela	*See-roo-eh-lah*
Pork	Cerdo	*Sehr-doh*
Potato	Patata	*Pah-tah-tah*
Refried beans	Frijoles refritos	*Free-hoh-lehs reh-free-tohs*
Ribs	Costillas	*Cohs-tee-yahs*
Rice	Arroz	*Ah-rohs*
Roast beef	Rosbif	*Rohs-beef*
Salad	Ensalada	*Ehn-sah-lah-dah*
Salmon	Salmón	*Sahl-mohn*
Salt	Sal	*Sahl*
Sandwich	Bocadillo	*Boh-cah-dee-yoh*
Sardine	Sardina	*Sahr-dee-nah*
Sauce	Salsa	*Sahl-sah*
Sausage	Salchicha	*Sahl-chee-chah*
Seafood	Marisco	*Mah-rees-coh*
Soup	Sopa	*Soh-pah*
Sour	Agrio	*Ah-gree-oh*
Steak	Bistec	*Bees-tek*
Sugar	Azúcar	*Ah-soo-cahr*
Sweet	Dulce	*Dool-seh*
Tea	Té	*Teh*

Tomato	Tomate	*Toh-<u>mah</u>-teh*
Tuna	Atún	*A-<u>toon</u>*

The Weather

What's the weather like today?	¿Cómo está el tiempo hoy?	*¿Coh-moh ehs-tah el tee-ehm-poh oy?*
What's it like outside?	¿Cómo está afuera?	*¿Coh-moh ehs-tah ah-fweh-rah?*
It is hot.	Hace calor.	*Ah-seh cah-lohr*
It is cold.	Hace frío.	*Ah-seh free-oh*
It is cool.	Hace fresco.	*Ah-seh frehs-coh*
The weather is nice.	Hace buen tiempo.	*Ah-seh bwehn tee-ehm-poh*
The weather is bad.	Hace mal tiempo.	*Ah-seh mahl tee-ehm-poh*
It is cloudy.	Está nublado.	*Ehs-tah noo-blah-doh*
It is sunny.	Está soleado.	*Ehs-tah soh-leh-ah-doh*
It is clear.	Está despejado.	*Eehs-tah dehs-peh-hah-doh*
It is windy.	Está ventoso.	*Ehs-tah vehn-toh-soh*
It is stormy.	Está tormentoso.	*Ehs-tah tohr-mehn-toh-soh*
It is raining.	Está lloviendo.	*Ehs-tah yoh-vee-ehn-doh*
It is snowing.	Está nevando.	*Ehs-tah neh-vahn-doh*
It's a heatwave.	Es una ola de calor.	*Ehs oo-na oh-lah deh cah-lohr.*
It is foggy.	Hay niebla.	*I nee-eh-blah*
It's raining pitchers/buckets!	¡Llueve a cántaros!	*¡Yoo-eh-veh ah cahn-tah-rohs!*
It's raining oceans!	¡Llueve a mares!	*¡Yoo-eh-veh ah mah-rehs!*
It's so cold it burns your skin!	¡Hace un frío que pela!	*¡Ah-seh oon free-oh keh peh-lah!*
I'm freezing!	¡Me estoy	*¡Meh ehs-toy cohn-heh-*

	congelando!	*lahn-doh!*
What heat!	¡Qué calor!	*¡Keh cah-lohr!*
It's an oven!	¡Es un horno!	*¡Ehs oon ohr-noh!*
I'm dying of heat.	Estoy muriendo de calor.	*Ehs-toy moo-ree-ehn-doh deh cah-lohr*

When in Trouble

Can I help you?	¿Puedo ayudarte?	*¿Pwe-doh ah-yoo-dahr-teh?*
Can you help me?	¿Puede ayudarme?	*¿Pwe-deh ah-yoo-dahr-meh?*
No problem.	¡Sin problema!	*¡Seen proh-bleh-mah!*
Can you say that again?	¿Puede repetirlo?	*¿Pwe-deh reh-peh-teer-loh?*
I don't understand.	No entiendo.	*Noh ehn-tee-ehn-doh*
I don't know.	No (lo) sé.	*Noh (loh) seh*
I have no idea.	No tengo ni idea.	*Noh tehn-goh nee ee-deh-ah*
I don't speak Spanish.	No hablo español.	*Noh ah-bloh ehs-pah-nyol*
Do you speak English?	¿Habla inglés?	*¿Ah-blah een-glehs?*
I'm lost.	Estoy perdido.	*Ehs-toy pehr-dee-doh*
What does ... mean?	¿Qué significa...?	*¿Keh seeg-nee-fee-cah...?*
My Spanish is bad.	Mi español es malo.	*Mee ehs-pah-nyol ehs mah-loh*
Can you speak more slowly?	¿Puedes hablar más despacio?	*¿Pwe-dehs ah-blar mahs dehs-pah-see-oh?*

Emergencies

Call the police!
>¡Llame a la policía!
>>*¡Yah-meh ah lah poh-lee-see-ah!*

Call an ambulance!
>¡Llame una ambulancia!
>>*¡Yah-meh oo-nah ahm-boo-lahn-see-ah!*

Call the fire department!
>¡Llame a los bomberos!
>>*¡Yah-meh ah lohs bohm-beh-rohs!*

Is there an extinguisher handy?
>¿Hay un matafuegos a mano?
>>*¿I oon mah-tah-foo-eh-gohs ah mah-noh?*

Help!
>¡Socorro!/¡Auxilio!
>>*¡Soh-coh-roh!/¡Ah-oo-xee-lee-oh!*

Fire!
>¡Incendio!/¡Fuego!
>>*¡Een-cehn-dee-oh!/¡Fweh-goh!*

I've had a car accident.
>He tenido un choque de automóvil.
>>*Eh teh-nee-doh oon choh-keh deh ah-oo-toh-moh-beel*

I have a flat tire.
>Se me pinchó la llanta.
>>*Seh meh peen-choh lah llahn-tah*

I need a tow truck.
>Necesito la grúa remolque.
>>*Neh-seh-see-toh la groo-ah reh-mohl-keh*

My husband/wife has had a heart attack.
>Mi esposo/a ha sufrido un ataque al corazón.
>>*Mee ehs-poh-soh/ehs-poh-sah ah soo-free-doh oon ah-tah-keh ahl coh-rah-sohn*

Does anyone know first aid?
>¿Alguien sabe de primeros auxilios?

¿Ahl-guee-ehn sah-beh deh pree-meh-rohs ah-oo-xee-lee-ohs?

Is there a doctor here?
¿Hay un médico aquí?
¿I oon meh-dee-coh ah-kee?

Her waters have broken.
Se le ha roto la bolsa de aguas.
Seh leh ah roh-toh lah bohl-sah deh ah-wahs

She is about to give birth.
Está a punto de dar a luz.
Ehs-tah ah poon-toh deh dahr ah loos

My son/daughter fell down.
Mi hijo/a se cayó.
Mee ee-hoh/ee-hah seh cah-yoh

She has a bad gash.
Tiene una lesión grave.
Tee-eh-neh oo-nah leh-see-ohn grah-veh

My father/mother can't breathe.
Mi padre/madre no puede respirar.
Mee pah-dreh/mah-dreh noh pwe-deh rehs-pee-rahr

He/She has something in his/her throat.
Tiene algo en la garganta.
Tee-eh-neh ahl-goh ehn lah gahr-gahn-tah

My wallet has been stolen.
Me han robado la billetera.
Meh ahn roh-bah-doh lah bee-yeh-teh-rah

I saw the perpetrator.
Vi al delincuente.
Vee ahl deh-leen-kwehn-teh

I didn't see him.
No lo vi.
Noh loh vee

There was one.
Había uno.
Ah-bee-ah oo-noh

There was more than one.

Había más de uno.

Ah-bee-ah mahs de oo-noh

Where can I find a lawyer that speaks English?

¿Dónde puedo encontrar un abogado que hable inglés?

¿Dohn-deh pweh-doh ehn-cohn-trahr oon ah-boh-gah-doh keh ah-bleh een-glehs?

There was a collision!

¡Hubo un choque!

¡Oo-boh oon choh-keh!

I need an interpreter.

Necesito un intérprete.

Neh-seh-see-toh oon een-tehr-preh-teh

Where can I find an American consulate?

¿Dónde puedo encontrar un consulado americano?

¿Dohn-deh pweh-doh ehn-cohn-trahr oon cohn-soo-lah-doh ah-meh-ree-cah-noh?

Hello operator, I need to make a collect call.

Hola, operador, necesito hacer una llamada por cobrar.

Oh-lah, oh-peh-rah-dohr, Neh-seh-see-toh ah-sehr oo-nah yah-mah-dah pohr coh-brahr

It's an earthquake!

¡Es un terremoto!

¡Ehs oon teh-reh-moh-toh!

Get under the door frame and protect your head.

Ponte debajo del marco de la puerta y protege tu cabeza.

Pohn-teh deh-bah-hoh dehl mahr-coh deh lah pwehr-tah e proh-teh-heh too cah-beh-sah

Health Issues

I need to see a doctor.
Necesito ver a un médico.
Neh-seh-<u>see</u>-toh vehr ah oon <u>meh</u>-dee-coh

Is there an emergency room close by?
¿Hay una sala de emergencias cerca?
¿I <u>oo</u>-nah <u>sah</u>-lah deh eh-mehr-<u>hehn</u>-see-ahs <u>cehr</u>-cah?

We need to see a pediatrician/dentist.
Necesitamos ver a un pediatra/dentista.
Neh-seh-see-<u>tah</u>-mohs vehr ah oon peh-<u>dee-ah</u>-trah/dehn-<u>tees</u>-tah

I'm sick to my stomach/I feel nauseous.
Tengo náuseas.
<u>Tehn</u>-goh <u>nah-oo</u>-seh-ahs

Could it be food poisoning?
¿Será una intoxicación?
¿Seh-<u>rah</u> <u>oo</u>-nah een-toh-xee-cah-<u>see-ohn</u>?

I've had diarrhea for 3 days.
Hace tres días que tengo diarrea.
<u>Ah</u>-seh trehs <u>dee</u>-ahs keh <u>tehn</u>-goh dee-ah-<u>reh</u>-ah

I have a pain in my chest.
Tengo dolor en el pecho.
<u>Tehn</u>-goh doh-<u>lohr</u> ehn ehl <u>peh</u>-choh

I'm dizzy.
Estoy mareado.
Ehs-<u>toy</u> mah-reh-<u>ah</u>-doh

I'm pregnant.
Estoy embarazada.
Ehs-<u>toy</u> ehm-bah-rah-<u>sah</u>-dah

It hurts here.
Me duele aquí.
Meh <u>dueh</u>-leh ah-<u>kee</u>

Do I need a prescription for this?
¿Necesito una receta médica para esto?

¿Neh-seh-see-toh oo-nah reh-seh-tah meh-dee-cah pah-rah ehs-toh?

Is this medication expensive?

¿Es costoso este medicamento?

¿Ehs cohs-toh-soh ehs-teh meh-dee-cah-mehn-toh?

Can I take this with…?

¿Se puede tomar esto con…?

¿Seh pwe-deh toh-mahr ehs-to cohn…?

Where is the nearest pharmacy?

¿Dónde está la farmacia más cercana?

¿Dohn-deh ehs-tah lah fahr-mah-see-ah mahs sehr-cah-nah?

I need ibuprofen.

Necesito ibuprofeno.

Neh-seh-see-toh ehe-boo-proh-feh-noh

I'm allergic to…

Soy alérgico/a a…

Soy ah-lehr-he-coh/ah ah…

I've twisted my ankle.

Me torcí el tobillo.

Meh tohr-see ehl toh-bee-lloh

I'm bleeding.

Estoy sangrando.

Ehs-toy sahn-grahn-doh

I've sprained my shoulder.

Me esguincé el hombro.

Meh ehs-gueen-ceh ehl ohm-broh

A spider bit me.

Me picó una araña.

Meh pee-coh oo-nah ah-rah-nya

Give me something for the pain.

Deme algo para el dolor.

Deh-meh ahl-goh pah-rah ehl doh-lohr

Do you have the antidote?

¿Tienen el antídoto?

¿Tee-eh-nehn ehl ahn-tee-doh-toh?

I have medical insurance.

Tengo seguro médico.

Tehn-goh seh-goo-roh meh-dee-coh

What kind of test are you going to run?

¿Qué tipo de análisis me van a hacer?

¿Keh tee-poh deh ah-nah-lee-sees meh vahn ah ah-sehr?

Could you help me fill out these forms?

¿Podría ayudarme a llenar el formulario?

¿Poh-dree-ah ah-yoo-dahr-meh ah yeh-nahr ehl fohr-moo-lah-ree-oh?

What is my copayment?

¿Cuál es el copago?

¿Kwahl ehs ehl coh-pah-goh?

How long do I have to stay at the hospital?

¿Cuánto tiempo debo quedarme en el hospital?

¿Kwahn-toh tee-ehm-poh deh-boh keh-dahr-meh ehn ehl ohs-pee-tahl?

Where is the reception?

¿Dónde está la recepción?

¿Dohn-deh ehs-tah lah reh-sehp-see-ohn?

How long is the estimated recovery time?

¿Cuál es el tiempo de recuperación?

¿Kwahl ehs ehl tee-ehm-poh deh reh-coo-peh-rah-see-ohn?

I'm afraid of needles.

Le temo a las agujas.

Leh teh-moh ah lahs ah-goo-has

Warning Signs

Warning.
Aviso.
Ah-bee-soh

Danger.
Peligro.
Peh-lee-groh

No smoking.
No fumar.
Noh foo-mahr

No entrance.
Prohibida la entrada.
Proh-ee-bee-dah lah ehn-trah-dah

No swimming.
Prohibido nadar.
Proh-ee-bee-doh nah-dahr

Wet floor.
Piso mojado.
Pee-soh moh-hah-doh

Under construction.
En obras.
Ehn oh-brahs

No returns.
No hay devolución.
Noh i deh-voh-loo-see-ohn

You are here.
Usted está aquí.
Oos-tehd ehs-tah ah-kee

In case of fire.
En caso de incendio.
Ehn cah-soh deh een-sehn-dee-o

Water unsuitable for drinking.
Agua no potable.
A-wah noh poh-tah-bleh

Slow down.
> Despacio.
> *Dehs-pah-see-oh*

Dangerous curve.
> Curva peligrosa.
> *Coor-vah peh-lee-groh-sah*

Keep your distance.
> Guarde la distancia.
> *Gwahr-deh lah dees-tahn-see-ah*

Fire extinguisher.
> Extintor de fuego.
> *Ehx-teen-tohr deh fweh-goh*

No entry. Authorized personnel only.
> No entrar. Sólo personal autorizado.
> *Noh ehn-trahr. Soh-lo pehr-soh-nahl ah-oo-toh-ree-sah-doh*

Do not sit here.
> No sentarse.
> *Noh sehn-tahr-seh*

Wet paint.
> Pintura fresca.
> *Peen-too-rah frehs-cah*

Wash your hands.
> Lávese las manos.
> *Lah-veh-seh lahs mah-nohs*

Smile, you are on camera.
> Sonría, usted está en cámara.
> *Sohn-ree-ah, oos-tehd ehs-tah ehn cah-mah-rah*

Communication

Do you use social media?
¿Tienes redes sociales?
¿Tee-eh-nehs reh-dehs soh-see-ah-lehs?

What's your handle?
¿Cuál es tu nombre de usuario?
¿Kwahl ehs too nohm-breh deh oo-soo-ah-ree-oh?

I sent you a friend request.
Te mandé solicitud de amistad.
Teh mahn-deh soh-lee-see-tood deh ah-mees-tahd

I like your profile picture.
Me gusta tu foto de perfil.
Meh goos-tah too foh-toh deh pehr-feel

Did you upload the photos to Instagram?
¿Subiste las fotos a Instagram?
¿Soo-bees-teh lahs foh-tohs ah Instagram?

I tagged you in the photos.
Te etiqueté en las fotos.
Teh eh-tee-keh-teh ehn lahs foh-tohs

I blocked him/her.
Lo/La bloqueé.
Loh/Lah bloh-kee-eh

He/She shared the post.
Compartió la publicación.
Cohm-pahr-tee-oh lah pooh-blee-cah-see-ohn

Do you have free wifi?
¿Tienen wifi gratis?
¿Tee-eh-nehn wifi grah-tees?

What's the network name?
¿Cuál es el nombre de la red?
¿Kwahl ehs ehl nohm-bre deh lah rehd?

Could you tell me the password?
¿Me podrías decir la contraseña?
¿Meh poh-dree-ahs deh-seer lah cohn-trah-seh-nya?

Internet is down.

Se ha caído internet.

Seh ah cah-ee-doh internet

I would like to sign into my email account.

Quisiera entrar a mi cuenta de correo electrónico.

Kee-see-eh-rah ehn-trahr ah mee kwehn-tah deh coh-reh-oh eh-lehc-troh-nee-coh

How can I access the app?

¿Cómo accedo a la aplicación?

¿Coh-moh ahx-seh-doh ah lah ah-plee-cah-see-ohn?

Would you help me set up the app?

¿Me ayudas a configurar la aplicación?

¿Meh ah-yoo-dahs ah cohn-fee-goo-rahr lah ah-plee-cah-see-ohn?

Do you use WhatsApp?

¿Tienes WhatsApp?

¿Tee-eh-nehs WhatsApp?

I added you to the group chat.

Te agregué al chat grupal.

Teh ah-gre-ghe ahl chat groo-pahl

Do you have a charger for my mobile phone?

¿Tienes un cargador para mi teléfono móvil?

¿Tee-eh-nehs oon cahr-gah-dohr pah-rah mee teh-leh-foh-noh moh-beehl?

Could you put the photos on a flash drive?

¿Puedes pasarme las fotos a un USB?

¿Pwe-dehs pah-sahr-meh lahs foh-tohs ah oon oo-ese-beh?

Talking on the Phone

What's your phone number?
¿Cuál es tu número de teléfono?
¿Kwahl ehs too noo-meh-roh de teh-leh-foh-noh?

May I talk to…?
¿Podría comunicarme con…?
¿Poh-dree-ah cohm-moo-nee-cahr-meh con…?

I'll call you.
Te llamaré.
Teh yah-mah-reh

Who is this?
¿Quién habla?
¿Kee-ehn ah-blah?

Please wait for a moment.
Espere un momento, por favor.
Ehs-peh-reh oon moh-mehn-toh, porh fah-vohr

Please call again later.
Por favor, llame de nuevo más tarde.
Porh fah-vohr, yah-meh deh noo-eh-voh mahs tahr-deh

Sorry, wrong number.
Lo siento, número equivocado.
Loh see-ehn-toh, noo-meh-roh eh-kee-voh-cah-doh

I cannot hear you clearly.
No te escucho bien.
Noh teh ehs-coo-choh bee-ehn

Hold the line, please.
Espere en la línea, por favor.
Ehs-peh-reh ehn lah lee-neh-ah, porh fah-vohr

The line is busy.
La línea está ocupada.
Lah lee-neh-ah ehs-tah oh-coo-pah-dah

The line is disconnected.
La línea está desconectada.
Lah lee-neh-ah ehs-tah dehs-coh-nehc-tah-dah

The telephone is ringing.
> El teléfono está sonando.
> *Ehl teh-leh-foh-noh ehs-tah soh-nahn-doh.*

Please answer the phone.
> Por favor, contesta el teléfono.
> *Pohr fah-vohr, cohn-tehs-tah el teh-leh-foh-noh*

I will call you back.
> Te devolveré la llamada.
> *Teh deh-vohl-veh-reh la yah-mah-dah*

Could you call this number?
> ¿Podrías llamar a este número?
> *¿Poh-dree-ahs yah-mahr ah ehs-teh noo-meh-roh?*

My number is...
> Mi número es...
> *Mee noo-meh-roh ehs...*

We talked on the phone.
> Hablamos por teléfono.
> *Ah-blah-mohs pohr teh-leh-foh-noh*

Yes, go ahead.
> Sí, dígame.
> *See, dee-gah-meh.*

Would you like to leave a message?
> ¿Le gustaría dejar un mensaje?
> *¿Leh goos-tah-ree-ah deh-jahr oon mehn-sah-jeh?*

I will call again later.
> Llamaré de nuevo más tarde.
> *Yah-mah-reh deh noo-eh-voh mahs tahr-deh*

Printed in Great Britain
by Amazon

69487526R00071